WOMEN
VOTE
PEACE

Women Vote Peace
Zurich congress 1919 – Zurich 2019

Documentation
of the 2019 re-enactment of the Zurich Congress 1919 of Peace Women and
collection of articles linking remembrance to perspectives for a feminist future.

Edited by IFFF, Internationale Frauenliga für Frieden und Freiheit,
the German Section of WILPF,
Women's International League for Peace and Freedom

This Book is part of the Project "Women Vote Peace"

Bibliografische Information der Deutschen Nationalbibliothek:
Die Deutsche Nationalbibliothek verzeichnet diese Publikation in der Deutschen Nationalbibliografie; detaillierte bibliografische Daten sind im Internet über dnb.dnb.de abrufbar.

Herstellung und Verlag: BoD – Books on Demand, Norderstedt
© 2019 Internationale Frauenliga für Frieden und Freiheit IFFF, Deutsche Sektion der Womens International League for Peace and Freedom WILPF

ISBN: 9783750402874

CONTENT

VORWORT UND GRUSSWORTE

VON DER VERGANGENHEIT LERNEN, VON DER GEGENWART INSPIRIERT UND VISIONÄR FÜR DIE ZUKUNFT BLEIBEN

Vorwort von Heidi Meinzolt

Vielleicht fragen Sie sich: Was hat eine Frauenfriedenskonferenz 1919 mit 2019 zu tun?

Lassen Sie uns 100 Jahre zurückschauen: Viele Frauen in europäischen Ländern und in der Welt bekommen zu diesem Zeitpunkt ihr Wahlrecht – unter historisch und politisch sehr unterschiedlichen Rahmenbedingungen und nach einem langen Kampf der Stimmrechtsbewegung und der Aktivistinnen. In manchen Ländern mussten jedoch die Frauen viel länger auf diesen Schritt zur Gleichberechtigung warten und viele Forderungen der Frauenbewegung sind bis heute nicht erfüllt oder sie sind zumindest (wieder) umstritten.

Der Kampf ums Stimmrecht war immer ein Schlüsselelement für Gleichberechtigung und Beteiligung an demokratischen Prozessen. Gleichzeitig erhoben viele Frauen ihre Stimme, um Kriege zu stoppen und den Frieden zu bereiten. Sie kamen teils aus einem sozialistischen Hintergrund, teils gehörten sie zu den radikal-bürgerlichen Pazifistinnen. Ihre Analyse der Ursachen von Krieg und Gewalt war eindeutig: sie prangerten die unheilige Allianz von Patriarchat, Industrie und Militär an. „Die Wirtschaft muss den Bedürfnissen der Menschen dienen, und nicht denen von Profit und Privilegien!" (Lida Gustava Heymann 1915). Das klingt auch nach über 100 Jahren feministischen Engagements sehr aktuell!

In 100 Jahren feministischen Kampfes wurde eine Menge erreicht: Das Frauenwahlrecht ist eine Selbstverständlichkeit – auch wenn ein gleichberechtigter Zugang zu Wahlen nicht überall gewährt ist, die Anzahl weiblicher Abgeordneter im Parlament teilweise rückläufig ist und fast nirgends auf der Welt 50% erreicht. Gender Mainstreaming hat Eingang in viele Leitlinien und in die politische Praxis gefunden – ein Gender Pay Gap und ein Defizit bei der Besetzung von Spitzenpositionen durch Frauen aber bleibt. Frauenrechte sind als Menschenrechte anerkannt – aber in der Umsetzung gerade sexueller und reproduktiver Rechte hapert es und lange sicher geglaubte Rechte werden nun wieder einem neo-konservativen Familienbild geopfert. Die Frauen-Frieden-Sicherheitsagenda, die auf Partizipation, Schutz und Konfliktprävention setzt, ist von der UNO anerkannt als unverzichtbares Instrument, nachhaltige Entwicklung und Frieden zu fördern.

Vergessen wir aber nicht, dass viele der Forderungen der frühen Frauenbewegung weit entfernt sind von einer adäquaten Umsetzung. Sie bleiben eine Vision, die inspiriert und antreibt im Sinne einer feministischen Außenpolitik: Abrüstung, Stopp von Rüstungslieferungen und Priorität für Konfliktprävention, gleichberechtigte Teilnahme an den Friedenstischen, ein Verständnis von Sicherheit als umfassende menschliche Sicherheit, die Klimagerechtigkeit, Zugang zu Ressourcen und Schutz der natürlichen Lebensgrundlagen verteidigt gegenüber kapitalistischen wachstumsorientierten Interessen und Ausbeutung. Das nennen wir Grundlagen einer feministischen Wirtschaftspolitik, die Care und Gemeinwohlorientierung ins Zentrum rückt. Daran arbeiten wir für die Zukunft.

Der Haager Kongress als Treffen der Internationalen Frauenstimmrechtsbewegung fand 1915 mitten im 1. Weltkrieg statt. 1136 Frauen aus 12 Ländern einigten sich auf die „Internationale Organisation für dauerhaften Frieden" und verabschiedeten wegweisende Resolutionen, die den Krieg beenden und weitere Kriege verhindern sollten: Die Beteiligung von Frauen an Entscheidungen, Abrüstung und gegen den Nationalismus gerichtete Prinzipien eines zukünftigen Völkerbundes. Eine prominente Frauendelegation konnte auf dieser Grundlage den Krieg zwar nicht stoppen. Aber ihre Forderungen zur Gründung des Völkerbunds flossen in die Vorschläge des amerikanischen Präsidenten Wilson ein. Als im November 1918 der Waffenstillstand verabschiedet wurde, mussten die Frauen auf ihren Plan verzichten, eine Konferenz parallel zu den offiziellen Verhandlungen in Paris/Versailles einzuberufen, und so kam der Kongress 1919 in Zürich zustande.

Die Frauen, die sich 1919 in Zürich zum ersten Mal nach dem schrecklichen Krieg wieder trafen, waren voller Emotionen und suchten Lösungen aus dem Kriegsdesaster für eine friedlichere Zukunft. Sie verlangten eine sofortige Einstellung der Hungerblockade angesichts des enormen Leidens der Zivilbevölkerung, insbesondere der Frauen und Kinder. Sie diskutierten ihre ersten Erfahrungen mit dem Wahlrecht und Gewaltfreiheit in der Erziehung und im Kontext revolutionärer Bewegungen. Universelle Abrüstung und der Völkerbund standen im Zentrum der Forderungen, um dem Nationalismus eine übergeordnete Entscheidungsebene entgegen zu stellen und dem Kriegshandwerk den Boden zu entziehen. Frieden musste die Komponenten von Gerechtigkeit und Freiheit enthalten. So wurde die Organisation in Zürich umbenannt in „Internationale Frauenliga für Frieden und Freiheit". Diesen Namen trägt sie heute noch.

Das hier vorliegende Rollenspiel ist eine Zusammenfassung des offiziellen Kongressberichts und konzentriert sich auf Schlüsselbeiträge der Protagonistinnen. Es soll an den Mut und die Ernsthaftigkeit der Diskussionen erinnern. Es soll der vorausschauenden Beständigkeit der Analysen und Forderungen Stimmen verleihen und damit eine Inspirationsquelle für Engagement und Aktivismus lokal bis global bilden. Über 50 Friedens-Aktivistinnen in historischen Kostümen spielten den Kongress von 1919 nach, am Original-Schauplatz, dem Hotel Glockenhof.[1]

Das Re-enactment wurde komplettiert durch 6 Workshops, in denen die 150 Frauen aus 22 Ländern, feministische Forderungen in den Kontext globaler Herausforderungen des 21. Jahrhunderts stellten: zu den Vereinten Nationen, Gleichberechtigung, Gewalt gegen Frauen, Friedenserziehung und globale Abrüstung, den Frieden wählen und eine Vernetzung der Friedensbewegung. Junge Frauen trugen die Forderungen symbolisch in die Zukunft.[2]

Damit ist der Bogen gespannt von Erinnerungsarbeit, der Kraft kontinuierlich weiter zu arbeiten und gemeinsam inspirierend für die Zukunft zu wirken.

Mein Dank gilt allen, die zu diesem Buch und zum Gelingen des Projekts mit großem ehrenamtlichen Engagement beigetragen haben, sowie dem "Europe for Citizens Programme der Europäischen Union als Sponsor. Für Interessierte und weitere Recherchen lohnt sich ein Blick auf die Website www.womenvotepeace.com mit zahlreichen Frauenbiographien, Artikeln zum Frauenwahlrecht, Filmen und Veranstaltungen.

1   Die Szenen sind in dem Film "The Return of the Dangerous Women" von Clapham Film Unit London festgehalten.
2   siehe Abbildung auf Seiten 51 ff

LEARNING FROM THE PAST, GETTING INSPIRED BY THE PRESENT AND BE VISIONARY FOR THE FUTURE

Preface by Heidi Meinzolt

You may ask yourself: What is the relevance of a Women's Peace Conference held in 1919 for 2019?

Let us look 100 years back: Women in many European countries and in the world get their voting rights in historically and politically quite different circumstances and after a long struggle of suffragettes and women's rights activists. In some countries, women had to wait much longer to finally being allowed to vote. Equality is nowhere perfectly implemented and/or partly questioned again.

Voting rights were always considered a key element for equality and participation in all democratic processes. At the same time, many women raised their voices to stop wars and to promote peace. They came partly from a socialist background, partly from the bourgeois radical pacifist women's movements and alliances. Their analysis of the root causes of violence and war was clear: it is the unhallowed alliance of patriarchy, industry and military. "The economy must serve the needs of the people and not those of profit and privileges" (Lida Gustava Heymann 1915). This sounds still familiar after a centenary of feminist commitment.

In 100 years women's/feminist activism, has reached a lot: Equal voting rights are taken for granted even if equal access to elections is not always guaranteed, if the number of elected women in some parliaments declines and nearly nowhere achieves 50%. Gender-mainstreaming is implemented in many political directives and practices – even if a gender pay gap remains, and we still deplore a deficit in high-ranking jobs for women eg. in key industries and also the academic sphere. Women's rights are recognised as human rights in many documents and international laws – even if the implementation of sexual and reproductive rights is still controversial and we experience a growing tendency of de-gendering debates and associate women with so called traditional family values. The Women-Peace and Security/WPS Agenda, focussing on the relevance of women's meaningful participation is regarded in the UN system as an indispensable instrument to reach sustainable development and sustainable peace.

But at the same time, many requests of the early women's movements are still not implemented. They remain a dream and a still inspiring vision in the sense of a feminist foreign policy: Disarmament, stop arms trade and priority for conflict prevention, equal participation in peace negotiations, security understood as comprehensive "human security", integrating climate justice, access to resources and protection of natural environments against economic interests of capitalist investors. The principle of a feminist economy, putting care economy and commons at the core, needs re-discussion and implementation.

The Hague congress as the biennial meeting of the International Woman Suffrage Alliance was held in 1915. 1136 women from 12 countries made it, despite enormous problems. It effected an organisation under the name of "International Committee of Women for Permanent Peace" and passed a series of resolutions to stop the war and prevent future wars. They clearly named the root causes of violence and war, demanded the enfranchisement of women on all levels, and disarmament. They formulated principles for a future League of Nations. A prominent delegation presented the options to politicians (and the pope) in many countries but could not stop the war. Ideas for the League of Nations instead re-appeared in the proposal of the American president Wilson after the war. In November 1918, when the armistice was arranged, the idea was to hold a women's congress at the same place as the official peace negotiations – Versailles. This turned out to be impossible and the congress was called in neutral Switzerland, 12. 5. 1919 in Zurich.

The women participating in the conference in 1919 in Zurich were very emotional, meeting for the first time after being separated by WW1 and reflecting on a way out of the political and social disasters caused by the war. They demanded an end to the hunger blockade, spoke about their first experiences with women's voting rights. They extensively discussed non-violence in education and in respect to the revolutionary movements they were experiencing in the month before the congress. A central issue was the request for the establishment of the League of Nations to prevent future wars and avoid nationalism, universal disarmament and the participation of women. At the end of the congress, they elected a delegation to bring these resolutions to the "Peace negotiations" of the men in Versailles.

Doors remained closed to the contributions of the now named Women's International League for Peace and Freedom/WILPF.

The following script of the play is a condensed version of the original congress report, highlighting the most significant contributions to the congress. Remembrance of the courage, the seriousness of discussions, and the foresighted consistency of the requests is a great inspiration for women's commitment and activism for Peace and Justice. More than 50 peace activists dressed in historic costumes performed the re-enactment at the original place, the "Hotel Glockenhof".[3].

Six workshops in which participated 150 women from 22 countries followed the play, allowing a transfer to present times with a gender lens on challenges in a globalised world in the 21st century:

Reclaiming the United Nations as a Peace organisation, creating equal opportunities, gender justice in full respect of the diversity of sex, race, colour, beliefs, diversifying initiatives for disarmament locally, nationally, Europe-wide and globally, strengthening peace education and environmental/climate justice in the spirit of SDGs, voting for women and peace, uniting capacities to resist to violence and fear. Young women presented symbolically the requests.[4]

This was excellent bridge building between remembrance, continuous empowerment and inspiration for the future.

Many thanks to all who contributed with enormous voluntary work to the book and the success of the whole project. Many thanks also to the "Europe for Citizens Programme" of the European Union for co-funding.

For interested people and further research, I strongly recommend the website www.womenvotepeace.com with numerous biographies of women activists, articles on women's voting rights in different political contexts, events in many countries and films.

---

3   *The scenes are part of the Film "The Return of the Dangerous Women by Clapham Film Unit, London.*
4   *See pictures on pages 51 ff*

GRUSSWORT VON NATASCHA WEY, PRÄSIDENTIN DER SP-FRAUEN DER SCHWEIZ

Liebe Frauen,

Vor 100 Jahren, vom 12. bis am 17. Mai traf sich hier in Zürich die Internationale Frauenliga für Frieden und Freiheit. Diese Woche war in der Wochenzeitung «Zeit» in einem schönen Artikel zu diesem Treffen zu lesen, den Pazifistinnen von damals sei klar gewesen, dass sie nicht nach ihrer Meinung gefragt würden, sondern dass sie ihre Forderungen selber zum Ausdruck bringen mussten. Sie forderten damals, die Rechte der Frauen in den Friedensprozess mit einzubeziehen, weil Gleichberechtigung als Grundpfeiler für gesellschaftliche Stabilität und einen nachhaltigen Frieden verstanden wurde.

Viele der Gleichberechtigungsforderungen der Frauen von damals sind auch heute noch nicht erfüllt. Ich werde das jetzt nicht im Detail aufzählen. Natürlich hat es Fortschritte gegeben. Das Stimmrecht wurde den Frauen in der Schweiz 1971 zugestanden. Für viele weitere Verbesserungen brauchte es den erfolgreichen Frauenstreik von 1991. Ich denke an die Einführung eines Gleichstellungsgesetzes, ich denke an die Umsetzung der Mutterschaftsversicherung, ich denke an den starken Anstieg der Frauenvertretung in der Politik in den 90er-Jahren und ich denke an die nötige und erfolgreiche 10. AHV-Revision, mit der Einführung der Pflege- und Betreuungsgutschriften in der AHV, so dass Frauen in der ersten Säule praktisch gleich hohe Renten haben wie Männer. Es gab Fortschritte, es brauchte dazu aber immer einen besonderen Effort der Frauenbewegung.

Seit etwa drei, vier Jahren ist die Frauenbewegung wieder lauter, wieder stärker wahrnehmbar. Lustigerweise sagen mir oft viele ältere Frauen: «Das hatten wir doch schon mal». Die Forderungen waren doch schon mal auf dem Tisch. Themen wie unbezahlte Arbeit, Care-Arbeit, Sexismus und die Ausbeutung von Frau und Klima sind auch diese Tage wieder auf der feministischen Agenda. In teilweise ähnlicher Manier wie in den 1970er-Jahren. Die Basler Geschlechterforscherin Franziska Schutzbach sagt sinngemäss: jede Generation Frauen müsse von neuem beginnen, weil es ein Merkmal des Patriarchates ist, Leistungen – auch historische Leistungen von Frauen – systematisch unsichtbar zu machen und zum Verschwinden zu bringen.

Die feministische Friedensbewegung ist für mich ein solches Beispiel. Welche Radikalität hatten die Frauen um Clara Ragaz in Zürich vor 100 Jahren! Wie visionär waren ihre Forderung, wie mutig ihr Anspruch für eine nachhaltige und friedliche Welt. Ich durfte vor etwa einem Jahr in Zürich an einer Tagung zur feministischen Friedensbewegung, die von Monika Wicki organisiert wurde, an einem Podium teilnehmen. Und ich habe mir schon da gedacht: das radikalste, das wir wohl in der heutigen, kriegerischen Welt fordern können ist Frieden. Und ich habe mir ebenfalls damals gedacht, dass ich mir wünsche, die feministische Friedensbewegung erfährt ein gleiches Revival und dieselbe Wiederentdeckung, die junge Frauen momentan in der Care- oder in der Sexismusfrage erleben.

Ich denke, eine Tagung wie heute ist ein erster, wichtiger Schritt dazu. Der Artikel in der «Zeit» ebenso. Wir sind momentan daran, den zweiten grossen Frauenstreik vorzubereiten. Er wird wieder am 14. Juni stattfinden. Ich wünsche mir sehr, dass dieser Tag auch ein Auftakt wird, dass viele jüngere Frauen in Anlehnung an die Vorkämpferinnen der feministischen Friedensbewegung ihre Forderungen auf die Strasse tragen. Und, wenn der Frauenstreik ein Erfolg wird, im Herbst auch viele Frauen in Bern stärker eingreifen in die Politik – in der Schweiz und in der Welt. Damit diese noch einige Zeit fortbesteht. Dafür brauchen wir die Lösungsansätze der Frauenfriedensbewegung. Ich wünsche euch eine gute und erfolgreiche Tagung.

INTRODUCTORY SPEECH OF WILPF INTERNATIONAL PRESIDENT JOY ADA ONYESOH

It is a great privilege and honor to stand be-fore you on this occasion, especially having travelled all the way from Nigeria, Africa, to attend this congress, reminding us the 2nd world congress of WILPF. This time we have over 130 women from 22 countries. I really want to appreciate everyone here today for the commitment to attending this enactment as a reminder of the importance of the work we have been doing for over a century. It is important that we are reflective of the times that we live in and our collective responsibilities towards world peace.

A hundred years ago, a hundred and thirty seven women gathered in Zurich to have the World Peace Conference. In those times, they were faced with wars and conflicts of different dimensions. Today the wars still persist but in very dynamic and evolving ways: wars that have to do with physical presence, and on the bodies and lives of women. In so many countries women and girls are targets just by virtue of being women and girls, so we are facing several attacks on different fronts. It is also very interesting to note that the fundamental pillars upon which the congress held in 1919 still has so much relevance today and has become the bedrock upon which a lot of these struggles that women are pushing and advocating for, such as incre-ased representation of women in peace processes and governance, quality representation, voices and rights. So sisters and brothers, while we enact this congress, and meet in our different workshops, I want us to reflect on our individual responsibility in relation to what is happening globally. In the world today, we have complex situations in which men and women are responsible in different ways. But I am so excited that we have our feminist peace agenda that is vested in alternative solutions to violence, wars, patri-archy amongst other root causes.

It is impressive to observe the inter-generational representation of women in this space and we need to intentionally look at ways of sustaining the movement. One of the many legacies of Women's International League for Peace and Freedom over the last hundred years and more, has been analyzing the root causes of many of these wars and conflicts and developing strategies for pushing alternative solutions.

I want us to reflect on the privileges we bring into the room and into our everyday life. This holds true for me especially as a woman of colour because I know that in 1919 most likely we didn't have any woman of colour but this has changed as a result of the fundamental principles that has brought women from all over the continent together. These principles are what has made WILPF expand into all the continents of the world today. We are united both in our common vision and struggle – even though the context varies across countries. But we remain united in the common framework for pushing for women's rights and ensuring women's participation at the table. Definitely the contexts are different but we should not allow man created barriers to divide or stereotype us and create the identities which we are living with today. I want us to take a deep moment to really reflect on these points because these are part of what the struggles we are seeing across the different continents are all about – Man created barriers.

We believe in the vision of peace. The Vote for Peace is as relevant today as it was hundreds of years ago and when we talk about voting for peace, it goes beyond the actual physical vote for peace. It encompasses the actions we do consistently every day that must speak to the realities of women across the world. We are interconnected and so, when we have insecurity in any part of the globe, it means everyone, everywhere is affected. We therefore all need to reflect on that even in terms of language. How do we couch our language when we speak to our sisters? We also need to look inwards as much as we look outwards and that is what WILPF has been doing across the different continents. Today we have seen the movement grow enormously in Africa. Why? Because the realities speak true for us – as much as it does for our sisters in the West.

Coming from Nigeria, where we just concluded our national elections, we saw increased violence and killings that has been unprecedented in the history of the country. Even as I stand here today, in the Federal Capital Territory of Nigeria, women are targeted and criminalized for being women. It is appalling that the State is sponsoring the abuse of women's rights and we are seeing a different kind of discrimination and stereotyping of women using state apparatus to make this happen. We therefore need to think through our strategies and how we can come together to win this war on the women's body and other kinds of physical wars happening everywhere.Most importantly, we must keep speaking the language and message of peace. Nonviolence has always been our tool and it cannot change. Violence cannot defeat violence and that is why we are resolutely and deeply convinced that our message of peace is resoundingly clear and that is what we must all forge forward with.

Throughout the rest of the days of this congress, I urge us to reflect on how our message of peace is being related and interpreted - bearing in mind that language has different connotations. I want us to be very mindful of the way our language is expressed and understood.We have a deep responsibility to all our sisters across different continents – our fore bearers and visioneers were mainly of European and Western origin and what they sowed in the past is what is speaking for us today. We have that responsibility to ensure that we move on with this vision irrespective of our context.

I am moved by our commitment and belief in this struggle for peace. We cannot relent or give up but rather, we must continue with our message of peace.

Thank you very much.

ZURICH CONGRESS 1919 AND RE-ENACTMENT IN 2019

THE WOMEN'S INTERNATIONAL CONGRESS, ZURICH 1919

By Ingrid Sharp

100 years ago in May 1919, 147 women from 15 nations gathered in Zurich just 5 months after the end of a devastating war that had raged across Europe for over four years, dividing nation from nation and storing up a tide of bitterness that women would have to work to overcome. Many of these women had met at The Hague in 1915 and had been working together since then to understand the causes of war and to find ways of preventing it in future. At the Congress, the Women's International League for Peace and Freedom (WILPF) was founded, a group still highly active today in the international politics of peace-building and post-conflict reconciliation.

Getting there

The women who travelled to Zurich in 1919 were brave, intelligent, hard-working and deeply committed to the cause of peace. Travel was not always straightforward – communications had been made more difficult by the war, trains were overcrowded and visas difficult to come by. The planned US delegation of 50 was reduced to 27 by their government's refusal to grant visas; Helena Swanwick of Great Britain was denied a visa in Paris and missed the first few days of the congress – the Parisian official responsible for issuing her visa was disturbed by the fact that she had been born in Munich: 'Don't worry', she responded acerbically 'it won't happen again'. Jeanne Mélin, travelling from France as one of only four representatives of that devastated nation, arrived late too and the Hungarian Rosika Schwimmer was unable to attend at all. Women from the defeated nations were not allowed to travel to allied countries and so the plan to hold the post-war congress in Paris had to be abandoned. An inter-allied congress of British, French and American women did take place in Paris, and delegates from Zurich travelled there after the end of the Congress to present the agreed resolutions to the diplomats negotiating the peace.

The devastation of war

British women travelling by train through the devastated regions of France and Belgium were confronted with the destruction of the war even before arrival in Zürich, where the the sufferings of the war years could be seen in the emaciated bodies and drawn, pallid faces of German and Austrian delegates, who were also too exhausted to follow the debate at times. Jane Addams, the American chair of the Congress, describes her shock at seeing what deprivation had done to the Austrian Leopoldine Kulka:

'She was so shrunken and changed that I had difficulty identifying her with the beautiful woman I had seen three years before. She was not only emaciated ... but her face and hands were covered with rough red blotches due to the long use of soap substitutes, giving a cruelly scalded appearance.' (Peace and Bread)

The women also encountered the dangerously malnourished Austrian children who had been sent to Zurich for feeding up – the sight of these undersized, subdued groups of children made a deep impression on the women as they saw for themselves what the continuing Allied food blockade meant in human terms. Images of the starving children were used in publications even years later by WILPF members, for example by British leader Helena Swanwick in The Roots of Peace (1938).

In the Congress Resolutions, Section I on famine and blockade condemned the continued starvation of enemy civilians as a 'disgrace to civilisation' and demanded a fair distribution of food to those in need and the raising of the blockade.

The Delegates

The largest groups were from America (27) Great Britain (26), Germany (25) and Switzerland (23). It was especially hard for women from France and Belgium to attend because of the continued resentment and hatred of the defeated enemy, which extended to German and Austrian women for several years after the war. Despite this, there was a small delegation from France and a Belgian woman, whose name is not recorded in the conference minutes, did in fact manage to attend.

Dismantling the mindsets of war

The Zurich women faced all the problems that made post-war co-operation between former enemy nations difficult, namely bitterness over lost lives and destroyed infrastructure, and from all the unresolved issues arising from invasion, occupation, and forced displacement. The defeated nations were destabilised by revolutionary unrest, the collapse of empire and acute economic insecurity as well as the continuing allied blockade.

Despite the many challenges of the post-war context and the enormous difficulties of overcoming the mindsets of war in defeated and victorious nations alike, the international women's organisations managed to rebuild their 'imagined communities' and integrate women of 'enemy' nations remarkably quickly and effectively. They used a highly gendered discourse of shared victimhood that stressed the unifying rather than the divisive nature of grief and bereavement, especially of mothers grieving for soldier sons. They used private and public gestures of sympathy and reconciliation to move beyond the cycle of bitterness and revenge that would make future wars inevitable and recognised that they had a common enemy: war itself. As Emily Greene Balch wrote in 1915 'the gains that either side makes are as nothing compared to their losses. [...] this all-outweighing fact is the intolerable burden of continued war.' [Balch in The Women at the Hague, 1915, p.55].

One of the most moving and dramatic moments of the congress was the spontaneous embrace between the German, Lida Gustava Heymann, and Jeanne Mélin and her hope that 'we women can build a bridge from Germany to France and from France to Germany, and that in the future, we may be able to make good the wrongdoing of the men.' After Melin had responded with a passionate resolve to oppose all militarism and hatred, the entire assembly rose and pledged themselves to 'do everything in their power towards the ending of the war and the coming of permanent peace.'

The Congress

The aim of the Congress was to comment on the terms of the peace treaty and work together to create conditions for a sustainable peace. The women had a copy of the draft terms of the Peace Treaty with Germany and the principles for the League of Nations and these were debated in detail before a response was agreed. As outlined above, the famine brought about by the war was roundly condemned as a disgrace to humanity, and neither the terms of the Peace Treaty nor the provisions for a League of Nations were viewed as effective instruments of peace. The women expressed their regret that 'the covenant of the League 'in many respects does not accord with the fourteen points laid down as the basis of present negotiations, contains certain provisions that will stultify its growth, and omits others which are essential to world peace.'

Their suggestions for improvement included allowing defeated nations to join the League; requiring immediate disarmament and abolition of conscription in all nations as a condition of membership and the guarantee of the rights of minorities and the right to self-determination of all nations, which would have effectively dismantled the empires of victorious nations. The key demand was of course full political rights and social and economic equality for women.

The concession that all the offices of the League of Nations should be open to women was seized on by the feminists, as it marks a real departure in women's international standing. The League became the focus of women's international activities in the post-war period and they took full advantage of the new opportunities. Women's organisations established a presence in Geneva, and set out to lobby the League, influence its structure and ensure that women were represented in its legislation. Women's work in and with the League established the precedent that women should be included in international affairs, helping to normalise international political engagement by women at a time when this was still highly contested at national level. In this way, women without the vote at home could be involved in international politics.

The women at Zurich did not wait for an invitation, but took the initiative, sending their critical comments and proposals to the men negotiating the peace in Paris, adding a women's charter that set out the central importance they attached to gender equality in all. What they put forward amounted to a declaration of human rights that included women and that applied to women regardless of cultural differences between nations and within religions.

Among the American delegation was Mary Church Terrell 1863-1954, the only woman at conference 'with even a drop of African blood' gave her speech in German, putting forward a resolution against discrimination on the grounds of race and colour

'We believe that no human being should be deprived of an education, prevented from earning a living, debarred from any legitimate pursuit in which he wishes to engage, or be subjected to any humiliation on account of race or colour.' [110][1]

WILPF may have been a product of its time and dominated by wealthy western Europeans, who were overwhelmingly white, but it was making a genuine effort to overcome imperialist mindsets and remove the barriers of race and class privilege.

Another highly contested topic was the revolutionary unrest that had resulted in regime change in Germany, Austria and Hungary. Some of the women had actively participated in them and many were convinced socialists, even communists, and a compromise had to be reached between those who felt that the revolutions had not gone far enough and wanted to share out private property and those like Aletta Jacobs who threatened to resign from WILPF if any such resolution was passed. In the end, the resolution recognised 'that there is a fundamentally just demand underlying most of these revolutionary movements. We declare our sympathy with the purpose of the workers who are rising up everywhere to make an end to exploitation', but they condemned all violent methods for achieving change.

Woman-centred peace

The women's analysis was highly gendered, and the major responsibility for the war was laid firmly at the feet of the men who had been responsible for the political mismanagement that had led to the catastrophic war. As Jane Addams recalled in 1922:

'Twenty-six governments of the world stood convicted of their own impotence to preserve life and property, they were directly responsible for the loss of ten million men in military service, as many more people through the disease and desolation following war, for the destructions of untold accumulations of civilized life.'[2]

In the imaginary of war, there was a clear division into women as life-givers and men as destroyers. This was based on women's observation of the world created by one-sided male rule, of which WW1 was just the worst and most recent example. Some of the women felt that men were capable

1   Numbers in brackets refer to the page number in the WILPF Report of the Congres
2   Addams, Jane 2010 [1922]. Peace and Bread

of change, but that they were being socialised and educated to a divisive and destructive version of masculinity, others believed that men were innately aggressive: men fought one another, women did not. Either way, male power was dangerous and threatened human happiness and fundamentally life on earth. Because of this, women's rights and peace were inextricably linked: without women's political and social influence society could not be reorganised to create the conditions necessary for a sustainable peace.

Nothing about the way the men were negotiating the peace in Paris had led the women to revise their low opinion of male diplomacy. Frida Perlen of Germany [80] argued that all the statesmen in Paris were in fact disqualified from making peace due to their complicity in militarism and their inability to prevent or halt the war. This view was amplified by Lida Gustava Heymann, who claimed that military men were in any case by definition incapable of making peace, and should not mix themselves up in matters they did not understand [205].Helena Swanwick [223] added:

'The men have reduced the world to this condition – do they admire it? Do they think it is beautiful?'

And for fellow Briton Ethel Snowdon 'If men can only settle their quarrels over the dead bodies of starved children, it is time that the men and women who think this is wrong got together to stop it.' [217]

The mess that men were making of the peace processes gave women the moral right and duty to intervene:

'We women, who are by nature creators and guardians of life, regard it as our duty in this moment of the world's history, after years of self-destruction, to undertake the establishment of a new world, to condemn in the most emphatic manner any attempt at re-establishing the principle of force, to recognise as the basis of future society the sacredness of life, and to proclaim the solidarity of humanity.' [72]

The women at the Congress put forward a woman-centred view of the world that saw wars as especially destructive of aspects of human life that were valued by women, and in which women were particularly invested. This included the destruction of men's bodies nurtured and cared for by mothers and wives, the destruction of homes and families and the communities which had provided food, shelter and safety. It also included more direct suffering such as displacement and sexual violence if male protection failed. Also, new weapons and strategies of war such as the starvation blockade, aerial bombardment and poison gas made women and children targets and a modern, industrialised war mobilised women as well as men.

They recognised that whether or not a society was at war, militarism entailed the subjugation of women as it was based on the argument of force versus reason. Also, money spent on military build-up diverted funds from areas of social welfare important to women such as education, health and the environment.

Significance and Legacy

The Women's International Congress at the Hague in 1919 and in Zurich in 1919 are highly significant. They show that even in the difficult circumstances of a global war, a minority within the women's movement in combatant and neutral nations reached across enemy lines and tried to maintain and even strengthen international bonds between women. These groups remained committed to what they saw as a womanly mission to influence the nations in the cause of peace, a mission that many continued to pursue after the war, using the League of Nations as a platform for international political action. They wanted to create a more stable, more interconnected world order based on principles of social and economic justice and with non-violent mechanisms for resolving conflict. The development of new and terrifying weapons and strategies of war that targeted civilian populations challenged the gendered division that separated men from women, combatant from non-combatant. Questions of war and peace could no longer be seen as issues separate from women's concerns: in a hostile and threatening world, the imagined community of internationally-minded women was urgently needed as a model for harmonious relationships between nations and as a platform for building a sustainable peace. The women at The Hague and Zurich challenged the male view of peace and offered a workable and intelligent alternative based on human rights, social, economic, gender, class and racial justice, education and legislation for peace within and between nations. WILPF was founded at the Zurich congress as a pioneering, radical force for peace that remains important and relevant today. Their analysis of the causes and ways to prevent war anticipated later developments and current thinking in Peace studies, International Relations as well as practical activism and is reflected in United Nations policies on gender, war and peace.

Further Reading

Addams, Jane, ([1922] 2010), *Peace and Bread in Time of War* (Memphis, Tennessee: General Books)

Addams, Jane, Balch, Emily Greene, Hamilton Alice (2003) [1915] *Women at the Hague. The International Congress of Women and Its Results* Urbana and Chicago: University of Illinois Press

Bussey, G. and Tims, M (1965) *Pioneers for Peace: Women's International League for Peace and Freedom, 1915-1965* WILPF, British Section

Heymann, Lida Gustava and Augspurg, Anita (1992) [1972] *Erlebtes Erschautes. Deutsche Frauen kämpfen für Freiheit, Recht und Frieden 1850-1940* Frankfurt am Main: Ulrike Helmer Verlag.

Resolutions of the 1st Congress, The Hague 1915 WILPF International [online] http://wilpf.org/wp-content/uploads/2012/08/WILPF_triennial_congress_1915.pdf

Resolutions of the Zurich Congress 1919 https://womenvotepeace.com/zurich-congress-1919/ and https://www.wilpf.org/portfolio-items/wilpf-congress-resolutions-and-proposals-1919/?portfolioCats=644%2C463%2C462%2C461%2C460%2C459%2C458%2C640

Rupp, Leila J. (1997) *Worlds of Women. The Making of an International Women's Movement* Princeton University Press.

Sharp, Ingrid (2013b) 'Feminist Peace Activism 1915 – 2010: Are We Nearly There Yet?' *Peace and Change* issue 2 April 2013 volume 38, pp.155-180.

Vellacott, Jo (2001) 'Feminism as If All People Mattered: Working to Remove the Causes of War, 1919 – 1929' *Contemporary European History* Vol 10, No 3, 375-394.

Wilmers, A. (2008) *Pazifismus in der internationalen Frauenbewegung (1914-1920): Handlungsspielräume, politische Konzeptionen und gesellschaftliche Auseinandersetzungen* Essen: Klartext Verlag.

WILPF [1915] *Report of the International Congress of Women: The Hague – The Netherlands, April 28th to May 1st 1915: President's Address : Resolutions Adopted : Report of the Committee visiting European Capitals.* (Nabu Public Domain Reprints).

WILPF (1919) *Rapport du Congrès International de Femmes Zurich Mai 12-17, 1919* Geneva: Ligue International de Femmes pour la Paix et la Liberté.

Wiltsher, Anne (1985) *Most dangerous women: feminist peace campaigners of the Great War* London: Pandora Press.

Programme

of the

International Congress of Women

ARRANGED by the

International Committee of Women
for Permanent Peace

ZURICH, May 12-17, 1919
Headquarters: Glockenhaus, Sihlstrasse 33, Zurich 1

The International Congress of Women which met at the Hague in 1915 resolved that «an international meeting of women shall be held in the same place and at the same time as the Conference of the Powers which shall frame the terms of peace settlement after the war, for the purpose of presenting practical proposals to that Conference».

*) A rule similar to that adopted at our Hague Congress excluding from the scope of discussion the relative national responsibility for the war or the relative national conduct of the war is adopted for the present Congress. In accordance with this plan the present Congress is meeting, although not at the place of the official Peace Conference. *

Monday May 12th 9.30-12 - Business Meeting at the Glockenhaus.
1. Opening of Congress.
2. Appointment of Interpreters and Recording Secretaries.
3. Address of welcome by Clara Ragaz, Chairman of Swiss Section.
4. Reply by Jane Addams, President of international Committee.
5. Financial report by Emily Balch.
6. Envoys to Governments in 1915: Report by Chrystal Macmillan.
7. Report of Credentials Committee and Roll Call.
8. Acceptance of Agenda.
9. Four years' work at headquarters: Dr. Aletta Jacobs.
10. Adoption of Rules of Order.
11. Appointments.

Monday, 2.30-4.30: Business Meeting at the Glockenhaus.
12. Information.
13. Reports and Experiences from National Sections of the International Committee of Women for Permanent Peace.

Monday, 8.15 p. m.: First Public Meeting in the Aula of the University. Addresses by Jane Addams, L. Kulka, Gertrud Baer, Margaret Ashton, Marguerite Gobat, Dr. Knischewsky, Florence Kelley, B. van Wulfften Palthe, Rosa Genoni.

Tuesday and Wednesday, 9.30-12 and 2.30-4.30 p. m.:
Business Meeting at the Glockenhaus.
14. Reports from National Committees. Continued.
15. Discussion of Resolutions to be submitted to the Official Peace Conference on terms of the Peace Treaty including the League of Nations and a Woman's Charter.

Tuesday, 8.15 p. m.: Public Meeting at the Aula, University.
Subject: Woman's Suffrage and Durable Peace. Addresses by Dr. Aletta H. Jacobs, Yella Hertzka, Charlotte Despard, Elisabeth Waern-Bugge, Eleanor Moore, Louie Rennett, Dr. Anita Augspurg, Jeannette Rankin, Henni Forchhammer.

Thursday, 9.30-12 and 2.30-4.30 p. m.: Business Meeting at the Glockenhaus.
16. Roll-Call.
17. The role of the Pacifists in the revolutionary movements.

Thursday, 8.15 p. m.: Public Meeting in St. Peter's Church.
Subject: Woman's Part in the League of Nations and other subjects. Addresses by Jane Addams, Lida Gustava Heymann, Else Beer-Angerer, Ethel Snowden, Mary Church Terrell.

Friday, 9.30-12 and 2.30-4.30 p. m.: Business Meeting at the Glockenhaus.

18. Education.

19. Future Work and Organisation of the International Committee.

Friday, 8.15 p. m.: Public Meeting in St. Peter's Church.

Subject: Woman's Part in the Reconstruction of the World. Addresses by Jane Addams, Helena Swanwick, Emmeline Pethick Lawrence, Blanche Reverchon, Vida Goldstein, Louise Keilhau, Dr. Helene Stöcker, Andrée Jouve, Alice Thacher Post, Vilma Glücklich.

Saturday, 9.30-12 and 2.30-4.30 p. m.:

Business Meeting at the Glockenhaus.

20. Future work and Organisation of the International Committee.

21. Recommendations to the National Sections.

22. Unfinished Business.

23. Close of Meeting.

Entertainments

Sunday, May 11 th, 8.30
**Reception of the Delegates at the «Meise»
organised by the I. W. C. P. P.**

Wednesday, May 14th, 6.30
Excursion and supper at the Uetliberg

Saturday, May 17th, 7.30
**Final banquet at the Tonhalle
organised by the Zürich Organisation Committee.**

RE-ENACTMENT

of the

1919
ZURICH CONGRESS

The Zurich Congress 1919 at the Glockenhof Hotel – historic photo

Close your eyes and imagine 100 years back in history.
We have the 11th of May 1919!
On the podium take place from left to right:
Rosa Genoni, Aletta Jacobs, Jane Addams, Chrystal Macmillan,
Clara Ragaz, Anita Augspurg

2019 Re-enactment of the Zurich Congress at the Glockenhof Hotel
Peace-women in historic costumes, even the hall decorated like 1919

Jane Addams: Welcome to our congress! We have many times hoped that  the day had arrived for this congress of ours which was to be convened at the time and the place of the Official Peace Conference. This was not possible, but now we are here together exactly in the moment when the Official Peace Conference has formally begun. Please rise and stand in silence in memory of those who had lost their lives in the war! Thank you!

These four years so full of anguish and sorrow for all the world have yet brought peculiar difficulties to the women assembled here as delegates to our 2nd congress. In every country, these women have represented a small group, which found itself opposed to the full tide of public opinion and of governmental action. Our committee members have demonstrated without doubt that the war methods are identical in all nations. While we approach our share with a full sense of complicity in the common disaster of the Great War, may we claim that we essay the task free from any rancorous memories of wilful misunderstanding or distrust of so-called enemies. We hope that the delegates will speak freely not only of their experiences but also of their hopes and of the methods, which they advocate in the difficult period of social and industrial re-adjustment always following war. Some of our delegates represent nations in which revolution with and without bloodshed, has already taken place – in Bavaria, Austria and Hungary - and we know that they stood against the use of armed force in such domestic crises as definitively they stood against its use in international affairs. We are to be congratulated that, having so soon come together under the shadow of the great war itself, we have an opportunity to hear thus early of the courageous and intelligent action taken by our own groups in the widespread war after the war. May we learn from life and from each other throughout this congress, which is now declared to be formally opened.

Clara Ragaz: Mit Dank und Freude heiße ich sie im Namen des Schweizerischen Frauenkommittees für dauerhaften Frieden, im Namen des Zürichischen Frauenkommittees in unserer Stadt willkommen! Es ist uns eine große Ehre, der Sammelpunkt zu sein für jene Frauen die inmitten der wildragenden Leidenschaften des Krieges die Fahne der Menschheit und 

der Menschlichkeit hochgehalten haben, und die auch jetzt wieder zusammenkommen, gemeinsame Grundlagen zu legen für einen künftigen Wiederaufbau und ein Zusammenwirken der Menschen. Wir können von diesem Kongress aus die Schuld nicht tilgen, die Erbitterung besänftigen, das Unrecht gut machen, aber in gemeinsamer Arbeit Lösung und Erlösung suchen. Namentlich die Frauen der kriegsführenden Länder haben das Odium der mangelnden vaterländischen Gesinnung auf sich nehmen müssen, obwohl sie ihm treu gedient haben, weil sie sich für übergeordnete Menschheitsziele eingesetzt haben. Ob uns das Frauenwahlrecht allein weiterbringt, ist nicht klar. Aber die Frau kann nur zu ihrem vollen Recht kommen, wo man nicht auf Gewalt sondern auf Recht setzt. Möge es uns vergönnt sein, etwas von dem zu verwirklichen, was wir erstreben, eine neue Einheit aufgrund einer lebendigen Vielgestaltigkeit. Möge es uns gelingen, hier im Kleinen zu verwirklichen, was im Großen leider der Verwirklichung noch fern zu sein scheint, einen Völkerbund an dem alle Nationen, die Großen wie die Kleinen, die Sieger wie die Besiegten miteinander arbeiten und möge dem zukünftigen Völkerbund beschieden sein, unter einer so weitherzigen und gütigen, klarblickenden und sicheren Leitung zu tagen wie wir es heute dürfen:

Jane Addams: I give now the word to the woman who had taken the burden of the work at the International headquarter for 4 years: welcome Aletta Jacobs. I am really sorry that it had not been possible to have our 2nd congress in Paris at the time as the peace negotiations going on in France. But we will do our work in the spirit of influencing the negotiations!

Aletta Jacobs: Dear women, I want to let you know what we have done between 1915, our congress in The Hague, and now 1919 from the international headquarter in Amsterdam: I have to thank a lot to the great help that I got from Rosa Manus and Chrystal Mac Millan!

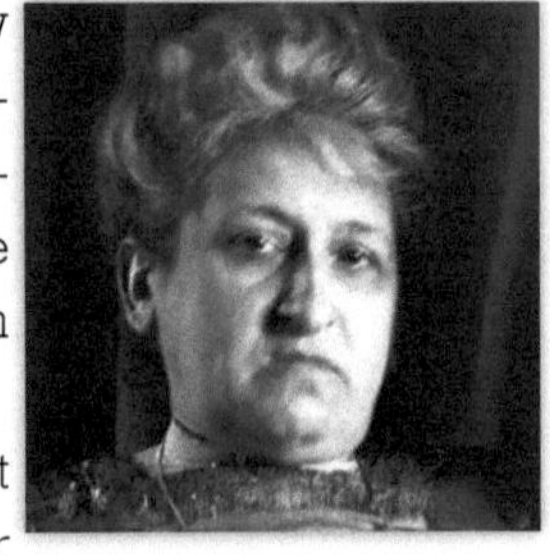

First, we have finished reports and sent them out to sections and important persons who either played a role in war or peace.

Second, we have published a newsletter! Here you see the "Internatioonaal".

Third, we have collected peace materials from all countries - and I have a lot here!

Fourth, I have taken personally the greatest pleasure of the letters of appreciation from the government of Cuba who wants us to come there to organise the Cuban women, from Argentina, Japan, Peru, China, Mexico, South Africa (where they could not found a section because the women preferred to continue to work with men) and also the Prince of Siam;

Jane Addams: The word has now Crystal Mac Millan from Scotland:

Crystal Mac Millan: Dear women, thank you for your presence here in Zurich. I have the honour to present you our agenda: First, we will talk about the Peace conference in Paris and what we recommend to the men negotiating there without us. Secondly we will talk about the League of Nations on the basis of our 2 Committees who have worked on it. Finally we will discuss about the our future work in the sections and on our international work.

If you agree with the agenda please raise your hands!

But at the beginning, I want to introduce our emergency resolution and I ask Emmely Pethick-Lawrence from the UK and Rosa Genoni from Italy to present the **resolution Nr. 1 on Blockade and Famine**

Emmely Pethick-Lawrence: This international congress of women regards the unemployment, famine and pestilence extending throughout Central and Eastern Europe and parts of Asia as a disgrace to civilisation and, urges the governments of the Allied Powers assembled in Paris to take immediate action.

Rosa Genoni: We request to lift the blockade immediately so that food and raw materials may be supplied to all the peoples in need

Emmely Pethick-Lawrence: To cooperate internationally in the just distribution of resources – food, raw materials, finances shall be transported immediately to those suffering from famine and pestilence

Rosa Genoni: To safe humanity and bring about permanent reconciliation and union of the peoples

Jane Adams: Thank you! Voted with unanimity! I want to interrupt the business now to make an announcement. A delegate from Australia has arrived after ten weeks of travel. Will Miss Moore come up on the platform and let us all look at her?"

Eleanor Moore: We from the Commonwealth affirm our sympathy with  thoughtful men and women everywhere who are earnestly seeking a way to consider the adoption of other means than armed force in the settlement of international differences! We are not many who could afford coming to Zurich, but we want to tell you that many are with you and that we – men and women - have twice voted to reject a conscription! On our letter, you see 500 signatures attached!

Chrystal Mac Millan: I now call the 2 Committees who have worked on the League of Nations! I know there is a lot to discuss, and some of you will say the proposal for the league of Nation is better than nothing – we can work it out, others think it is unacceptable, a too idealistic proposal! Committee A will be reported by Lucie Mead from the US:

Lucie Mead: At this critical moment, when the fate of millions is trembling in  the balance, when famine, despair and chaos threaten a large part of the world, we believe that women of broad vision help make the League of Nations a vehicle of life. In this acute crisis, it is the best available alternative to the old system of alliances, balance of power and war! While striving as earnestly as possible for the attainment of an ideal world organisation, we believe that the people of the world should accept this Magna Charta, which make an enormous advance upon the previous anarchic relations existing between States. This congress should use its influence towards the development of a peaceful evolution in international relations.

Mac Millan: Committee will be presented by Charlotte Despard.

Charlotte Despard: The principles are laid down by the allied statesmen. The financial clauses will provoke suffering enough to cause anarchy and ruin for generations. I speak of the people and not of the governments. There are no signs of disarmament of Britain and the US. No to the principle of force, to recognize as the basis of a future society the sacredness of life and the solidarity of humanity: It must be equally vital that there must be total international disarmament, prohibition of the manufacture of munitions of war. We need a universal system of law to settle international legal questions and to prevent disputes. There is the need to create a plan of world economy satisfying the world's needs, the exclusion of all private profit, the exclusion of child labour, inclusion of exchange between countries of teachers and pupils! Out of this proposed treaty in Versailles – there is no hope for permanent Peace!

Jane Adams: Let's open the discussion: I call first Cor Ramondt-Hirschmann from the Netherlands:

Cor Ramondt-Hirschmann: We women must seek to realize the ideal thing and by working together we may overcome difficulties and not allow fear, doubt and distrust.

Yella Hertzka: Ich komme aus einem sehr kleinen Land, aus Österreich, aber ich komme mit vielen Erfahrungen und ich sage euch: Frauen dürfen sich nicht mehr auf Kompromisse einlassen – die Frauen haben nicht mitzugehen in den Fußstapfen der Männer, wir haben nicht Regierungen zu folgen – wir haben Regierungen zu wählen, so wie sie uns für unsere ferne Zukunft vorschweben – nicht um Konkurrenz zwischen den Nationen geht es, sondern gegenseitige Hilfe! Wir brauchen uns nicht zu bekümmern, ob vielleicht in Paris irgendjemand von der Völkerbundkonferenz sagt: Oh diese Frauen sind lächerlich! Wir in Österreich waren auch lächerlich, als wir von Verständigungsfrieden sprachen, aber 1917 lachte man nicht mehr!

Leopoldine Kulka: I am also from Austria, and I fully agree with Yella!

Anita Augspurg: Wir haben nicht das gutzuheißen, was die sogenannten praktischen Staatsmänner in Paris tun, sondern das festzustellen, was die Frauen für richtig halten. Aber verehrte Versammlung, es hängt von der Entscheidung ab, die wir Frauen treffen, ob wir in Zukunft das Vertrauen der Welt genießen als eine Korporation die hohe und neue und ideale Anschauungen für die Welt auszuarbeiten hat.

Frieda Perlen: Ich bin ebenfalls aus Deutschland. Ich versetze mich zurück an den Beginn des Krieges am 4.August 1914. Damals habe ich gesehen, welcher Wahnsinn unter den Menschen meines Vaterlands ausbrach, ich habe gesehen, dass die Leute verrückt wurden und nur wenige ruhig Blut behalten haben. Aber wir Frauen sind dazu berufen, die neue Zeit zu bringen. Die Staatsmänner, die sich mit Blut befleckt haben, haben weder das Recht noch die Fähigkeiten, den Militarismus niederzuwerfen. Und, nichtwahr, wozu sind die Menschen in den Krieg geschickt worden…wir sind alle angelogen worden. In den Krieg gezogen sind die Menschen für den internationalen Kapitalismus! (Applaus!). Wir wollen dem internationalen Kapitalismus nicht noch einmal auf die Füße helfen. Lassen sie unsere Ideale rein aus diesem Kongress gehen.

Mien van Wulfften-Paltheé: I am from the Netherlands: Now that we have woken up, we would commit an even greater crime if we don't seek for the means to avoid such a catastrophe in the future.

Aletta Jacobs: I give the word to our Hungarian colleague Vilma Glücklich:

Vilma Glücklich: If the long row of experiences convinces the conscious woman about that the men see a partner in her with equal right and equal work; if the men understand women's work not only from economic but also from ethical point of view, if the men acknowledge only one kind of moral code which is obligatory for both gender, if it won't be necessary for women's whole organizations to fight against the stubbornness of mail egoism and concealed preconceptions and battle for getting places of productions – then women's independent organizations will become unnecessary. No longer people will deal with pulling each other back, limiting each other's freedom, but cooperation will fulfil their work, and make their life more beautiful and happier. Unfortunately, we are very far from it today.

Marta Larsen: I am from Norway – Sorry that we came late, but I have to mention clearly that we do not admit war as a means of settling differences between people.

Cor Ramondt-Hirschmann: I propose the following to unite the ideal and the practical: This international congress of women records its satisfaction that the idea of a League of Nations has now become almost universally accepted. But it regrets that the existing draft is not democratic. It is a League of Conquerors against Conquered, it tacitly maintains the

old discredited system of the balance of power and
therefore it will not achieve its declared purpose of
saving the world from future wars; there must be
international disarmament by mutual agreement;
since permanent peace can be ultimately secured
only by complete disarmament , by abolition of
conscription in all countries and by safeguarding

of the political and economic rights of all nations and races.

Leopoldine Kulka: Ich bin meinen Vorrednerinnen außerordentlich dank-
bar, dass wir auf den Punkt des Wirtschaftssystem zu sprechen kommen, sonst gibt es keinen dauerhaften Frieden: Weizen wird gebaut,
damit die Menschen Geld verdienen – sollte er nicht gebaut werden,
damit die Menschen zu essen haben? Für uns Frauen ist das doch keine Frage. Unser ganzes Wirtschaftssystem muss
von den Bedürfnissen und der Existenzsicherung
eines Jeden Einzelnen ausgehen. Das sind nicht
Ideale, sondern Prinzipien! Wir wollen, dass die
Entwicklung zu einer sozialistischen Weltwirtschaft
auf friedlichem Weg vor sich gehen möge

Chrystal Mac Millan: This congress of women holds
that the peaceful progress of the world can only be assured when the
common interests of humanity are recognised in the League of Nations
for the promotion of international cooperation and based upon a system
representative of the people, upon which every nation is represented,
which aims at international disarmament, which provides machinery
for the administration of justice. The congress records its satisfaction
that the idea of a League of Nations, which in 1915 was still regarded as
impracticable, has become so widely accepted. Even the admission of
women to all positions. This congress declares that it is essential to the
success of the League of Nations to be set up under the treaty of Peace,
if it is to be an instrument of peace and capable of future development:
Membership should be from the beginning be open to all autonomous
States which express their willingness to become members; the conditions of disarmament should be applicable on the same terms to all the
States joining; all nations should have free access to raw materials and
equal trading opportunities and have the same right to protection. And
finally, we urge the Peace Conference to include a Women's Charta.

Margaret Ashton: The Peace treaty must contain a real women's Charta with different principles: Suffrage should be granted to women and their equal status with men upon legislative and administrative bodies, nationally and internationally recognised.

Ellen Wilkinson: It must also contain the Protection of

the law against slavery. All customs, weather social, religious, or domestic which entail the sale, barter or disposal of women and girls in marriage or otherwise, should be decreed to be contrary to international law and the law against slavery should be applied in such cases.

Theodora Mary Wilson: Trafficking in women should be suppressed.

Leonore Selenka: Frauen sollten den gleichen Lohn für gleiche Arbeit erhalten. Alle Berufe, Erziehung – auch die technischen, sollten Frauen offen stehen!

Ada Salter: Legal and economic equality between husband and wife should be established with equal rights of heritage

Anita Augspurg: Mir kommt es darauf an, dass die Frauen überall mitzusprechen haben und dass ihr Urteil gehört werden muss. Denn die Männer erörtern alles mit einem kolossalen Aufwand an Wissenschaftlichkeit und bringen nie auch nur die bescheidenste Dosis Vernunft an die Oberfläche!"

Aletta Jacobs: Let me repeat our main points: we welcome the League of Nations, but clearly say that to secure world peace , we need more: immediate disarmament, no obligatory military service, democratic elections for the executive, stop child labour, full voting rights and co-decision for women and men, equal pay for women and men, stop trafficking, equal participation of women and men in the referendum for the treaty. Accepted!

Jane Addams: I give the word now to our Bulgarian or Ukrainian representative:

Lydia Schischmanov: I bring you greetings from Bulgarian women. We had not desired the war. While the men were away, the women took care of all the work that had to be done, specially the farm work. It was they who fed Bulgaria during the years of war. This was recognised by the press and the parliament. Now the Bulgarian women are with us like the women of all countries that have suffered so long, for a durable peace.

Jane Addams: I am calling now for a resolution on the right to asylum and the protection against deportation

Lucie Mead: For years and years in the US we invited the oppressed of all the world! But now in time of war, when this policy would have been of greatest importance to maintain the right of asylum, we have suddenly made new regulations and are driving people out and to restrict totally immigration. I believe that it is a duty of enlightened women to  combat these tendencies They are part of the disease of war.

Lida Gustava Heymann: This is very important. I put this immediately to a vote!

Aletta Jacobs: We want to open the debate now on pacifist-revolutionary movements. I ask Helen Crawford from the UK to speak!

Helen Crawford: In view of this manifestation of force on the part of the authorities, it is difficult to advice or counsel against force on the part of the people. Nevertheless, I believe, that the Women's International League which had counselled against the use of force in the settlement on international disputes could do no other than counsel against its use nationally. My colleague Annot Robinson will explain more.

Annot Robinson: Facing widespread revolutionary changes at a time when the passions of hatred and fear and the habit of violence have been fostered by a world war we urge upon our sections to cooperate in seeking methods by which the energies enlisted in creating a new industrial order may do their work in constructive and vigorous ways without violence! Pacifism desires to find methods and may find ex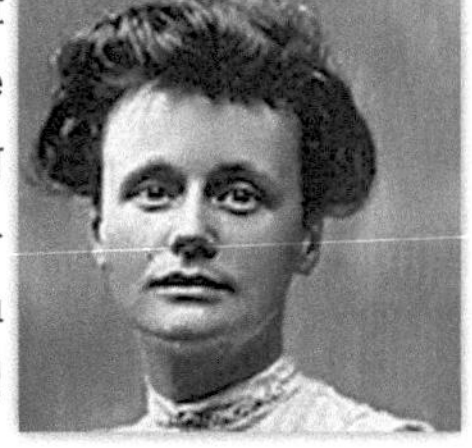pression without bloodshed. And believe in human spirit! What are our German and Austrian colleagues telling us about their experiences?

Anita Augspurg: Wir in Deutschland haben sofort nach der Verkündigung unserer hoffnungslosen Niederlage das militärische System zur Seite zu räumen versucht. Wir haben unsere Regierungen beseitigt und

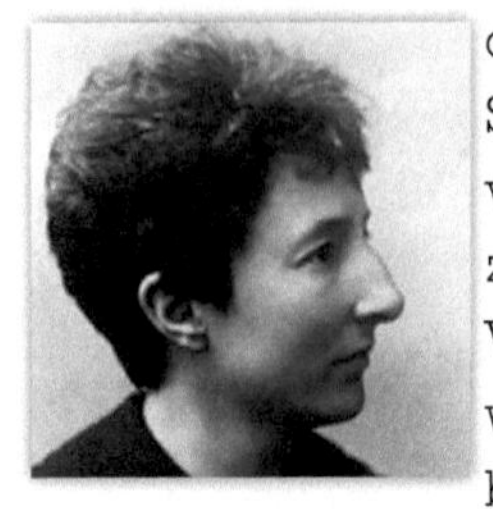

die Republik unter der Herrschaft des sozialistischen Systems erklärt. Es war eine natürliche Folge der Revolution, dieses kapitalistische System aus der Welt zu schaffen, das die Ressourcen nur dem Militär zur Verfügung stellt. Denn die Völker sind nicht mehr willens sich für den Kapitalismus knechten und ausbeuten zu lassen. Wir (in Bayern – mit dem höchsten Kulturstand) haben ganz unblutig versucht, den Männern Waffen und Munition unzugänglich zu machen. Sonst ist unsere Macht als Frauen dahin. Ich rufe ihnen zu, streben sie danach, den Gebrauch der Waffen zu unterdrücken. Ich weiß, dass das für uns Frauen unendlich schwer ist. Aber ich weiß auch, dass die Macht der Frauen vollständig dahin ist in dem Augenblick, da die Männer die Waffen in der Hand haben!

Lida Gustava Heymann: Ich will noch kurz ergänzen: Wir haben in Bayern

beantragt, dass an allen maßgeblichen Stellen Frauen mitarbeiten. Das hat z.B. dazu geführt, dass das Revolutionstribunal ohne Todesstrafe war. „Rechtsprechung nach wahrer Menschlichkeit" forderten wir ein, und immer wieder Vermittlung zwischen den sich immer mehr sich verhärtenden Fronten. Das war nicht nutzlos und sollte immer wieder bedacht werden - auch wenn am Schluss bei der brutalen Niederschlagung der Revolution der Blutzoll sehr hoch war.

Constanze Hallgarten: Ich bin ebenfalls aus München und möchte noch ergänzen: Wir haben viel erreicht in den letzten Monaten, aber es sind auch viele unserer Forderungen noch nicht erfüllt! Wir Frauen in Deutschland und Österreich konnten im Januar immerhin zum ersten

Mal zur Wahl gehen! Obwohl die Wahlbeteiligung der Frauen bei 80 % lag, haben wir Frauen in Deutschland nur wenige Sitze in den Parlamenten erhalten! Wir waren zu wenige, um in München trotz aller Bemühungen und Vermittlungen den Bürgerkrieg, das Chaos und die Gewalt zu verhindern - gerade vor unserer Abreise hierher haben wir die letzten blutigen Gefechte erleben müssen. Wir brauchen Mitspracherecht in allen Gremien, um solche Gewaltausbrüche zu verhindern! In Bayern hat uns Kurt Eisner, für den wir Frauen gleichberechtigt waren, darin unterstützt. Auch er wurde brutal ermordet.

Yella Hertzka: Please all participants stand up to commemorate Eisner, revolutionary leader in Bavaria for a peaceful revolution! Ich bedauere auch, dass keine Russinnen da sind, denn ich bin der Überzeugung, dass die Nachrichten, die wir aus der Presse bekommen nicht immer glaubwürdig sind. Unsere Revolution war weitgehend unblutig. Eines Tages sagten wir zu Karl von Habsburg: Geh! Und wir waren eine Republik. Wir in Österreich haben versucht, den Kapitalismus sukzessive abzubauen, durch Sozialisierung von Budgets und Schulen. Wir haben die Todesstrafe abgeschafft und Großgrundbesitzer enteignet, die Kleinbauern sollen erhalten werden. Mit der Sozialisierung der Betriebe ist es noch etwas schwieriger, da sie auf Grund des Krieges völlig herabgewirtschaftet sind. Die Frauen haben bei dieser Bewegung sehr viel geschafft und waren auch im Gemeinderat und im Parlament aktiv.

Dr. Helene Stöcker: In einem Punkt bin ich nicht ganz der gleichen Meinung; ich glaube nicht, dass die Kriege zwischen den Völkern nur die Konsequenz des Kapitalismus sind; sicherlich entscheidend, aber auch falsche Ideologien sind daran schuld. Wer gegen den Krieg gegen andere Völker ist, muss als Pazifistin auch darauf einwirken, dass die Waffen  nicht im Inneren eingesetzt werden. Bei uns in Deutschland haben sich Sozialdemokraten zum großen Krieg bekannt und Kommunisten versucht eine neue Wirtschaftsordnung mittels Gewalt herbeizuführen, deswegen ist es schwierig, mit ihnen zu verhandeln. Wir glauben also, dass der Sozialismus nicht gleich den Weltfrieden bringt. Wir müssen die Überwindung des Bösen insgesamt einschlagen! Wir müssen für eine Verschmelzung von Sozialismus und Pazifismus eintreten!

Leopoldine Kulka: Gerade wir Frauen, die wir immer wieder den Wunsch haben, dass alle Kinder, alle Schwachen, alle Unterdrückten ihre Bedürfnisse finden, sagen, dass es in der Welt keine privilegierten Klassen geben darf – die Menschheit ist eins!

Lucie Mead: We re-assert our belief in the methods of Peace. We have to prepare the wealthy and privileged classes to give up their wealth and privileges without struggle so that the change from a competitive system of production for private profit is possible into a cooperative system of production for human happiness!''

Martha Larsen: I want to tell you that Peace education has to start very early,  our history teachers should not just tell about wars and heroes, but tell about culture and diversity! We need health education not to form strong warriors but to resist; we need more foreign languages, international students exchange, summer courses, we need also media – not just to fulfil national-chauvinistic duties! Yes, we need the development of an international spirit, world citizenship, women as world citizens to be trained.

Emmeline Pethick-Lawrence : War is hypnotism, which takes possession of a people, and all possible channels artificially foster the hatred engendered by war. War could not exist if there would not be suppression of the truth! I ask you all to realise your personal responsibility in this matter. If you do so, we can face the future with hope!

Helena Swanwick: Peace is an active quality, is not a mere denial of war. Peace is the readiness to use your brains and your goodwill to solve every problem if it arises. You have to find where the root of the problems is, see where the oppression lies, where injustice is done. You need knowledge, training, and discipline and be organised. So the future lies in the hands of these young committed women!

Gertrud Baer: Verehrte Frau Präsidentin, sehr geehrte Versammlung: Ich  bin wahrscheinlich eine der jüngsten Vertreterinnen hier auf dem Kongress. Ich möchte ihnen sagen, dass in Deutschland eine Jugend bereit, mit allen Kräften am neuen Aufbau der Gesellschaft zu sprechen. Insofern grüße ich von hier aus auch die internationale Jugend! Bitte stimmen sie mir zu!

Mary Church Terrell: In a congress talking about the question of Peace, at  least one representative of a woman of colour should be present. No women on earth are more committed to peace than women of colour, in the US, in Africa or living on an island. In this war, organised by white men, many men of colour had to fight. Permanent peace is only possible if racism stops! The values of a human being are independent of their class, race and religion. We believe no human being should be deprived of an education, prevented from earning a living, debarred from any legitimate pursuit in which he wishes to engage, or be subjected to any humiliation on account of race or colour. We recommend that members of this Congress should do everything in their power to abrogate laws and change customs, which lead to discrimination against human beings on account of race or colour.

Aletta Jacobs: Who is in favour of this resolution, please raise your hands! Unanimous adoption!

Jeanne Mélin: J'arrive, I made it at last, mes amies, bonjour!

Lida Gustava Heymann snatches up the big bunch of roses from the table and runs down from the stage to meet Jeanne. They embrace. The delegates rise to their feet clapping:
A German woman gives her hand to a French woman and I say in the name of my section that that we women can build bridges and that in the future we may be able to make good the wrongdoing of the men – we women of the world who all feel alike, who want to protect and not to destroy, we shall always understand each other.

Jeanne Mélin: Au lendemain de la catastrophe, je regarde avec crainte et non sans angoisse les hommes d'Etats préparer de nouvelles guerres. Notre féminisme n'est pas la lutte contre l'homme il veut le bonheur de l'humanité il veut la place pour chaque être humanin travaillant à l'amélioration du sort de tous, dans la mesure de ses forces, de son  intelligence, de ses facultés. Les femmes sauront imposer leurs conceptions du droit à la vie, en dénoncant le militarisme destructeur, soutient de toutes les oppressions!

Yella Hertzka: Jeanne Melin hat schon die Einleitung gegeben zu dem was ich Ihnen sagen will. In diesem Saal sind wir in einer Art Oase in der Wüste. Wir haben beschlossen, die Zukunft aufzubauen. Aber wir müssen die Menschen überzeugen. Lassen sie uns einen Generalstreik der Frauen gegen den Krieg beschließen! Das ist unmöglich sagen viele? Ich frage ja auch nicht, wenn ich einen Baum pflanze, ob ich einmal darunter im Schatz sitzen kann. Es gibt in Zukunft gar keine anderen Mittel gegen den Krieg, als dass wir unsere Arbeit niederlegen, indem wir unser Geld der Kriegsunterstützung verweigern. Wir tragen den Menschheitsgedanken durch die Welt!

Frieda Perlen: Ich habe immer gesagt, wenn wir Frauen in allen Ländern und in allen Städten zu Hunderttausenden auf die Straße gegangen wären und wenn wir am 4. August 1914 alle gesagt hätten, wir lassen unsere Kinder nicht ziehen, glauben sie hätten die Männer es gewagt mit Maschinengewehren gegen hunderttausende von Frauen vorzugehen? Und darum sage ich, wir haben große Schuld auf uns geladen. Eine Befreiung kann es nicht im Heldentum, sondern nur mit geistigen Waffen geben.

Martha Larsen: Yes, we women need an international agreement to refuse war in money, work and propaganda!

Aletta Jacobs: And so the resolution to organise for a women's strike is adopted!

Anita Augspurg: Unser Kongress fordert dann den Kongress der Sozialisten, der im August 1919 in Luzern geplant ist, auf, dieselbe Resolution zu verabschieden! Da müssen sie dann alle Frauensolidarität zeigen! Nie wieder sollen Sozialdemokraten den Ausbruch eines Krieges dulden, sondern bei jeder Gefahr des Weltfriedens die Unterstützung durch Streik, Dienstverweigerung und Kreditverweigerung mittragen.

Aletta Jacobs: Before we end this congress, let us vote for our delegates to Paris: We have 17 nominations. Please put your vote in the box: Could you help and read the result Gertrud!

Gertrud Baer: Charlotte Despard 65 votes, Rosa Genoni 47 votes, Chrystal Mac Millan 46 votes, Clara Ragaz 38 votes. The delegation will be completed by Jane Addams and Gabrièle Duchène!

Jane Addams: We can say to one another that we have met and discovered that even after a great war, women from belligerent countries can come together, not in a pretended good will, not in a mere outside sentimentalism, but in genuine friendship and understanding. Wether we fail or not, we know that we have the clue and the military way has to come to an end. **We meet again!**

The protagonists from 1919

Jane Addams .... US
Lucie Ames Mead .... US
Margaret Ashton .... UK
Anita Augspurg .... D
Gertrud Baer .... D
Mary Church Terrell .... US
Helen Crawfurd .... UK
Charlotte Despard .... UK
Rosa Genoni I
Vilma Glücklich .... HU
Vida Goldstein .... AUS
Constanze Hallgarten .... D
Yella Hertzka .... A
Lida Gustava Heymann .... D
Aletta Jacobs .... NL
Josefine Kulka .... A
Martha Larsen .... NO
Chrystal Macmillan .... UK
Jeanne Mélin .... F
Eleanor Moore .... AUS
Frieda Perlen .... D
Emmeline Pethwick Lawrence . UK
Clara Ragaz .... CH
C. Ramondt Hirschmann .... NL
Annot Robinson .... UK
Mrs Rods .... UK
Ada Salter .... UK
Lydia Schischmanov .... BG
Leonore Selenka .... D
Helene Stöcker .... D
Helena Swanwick .... UK
Ellen Wilkinson .... UK
Theodora Mary Wilson .... UK
R. van Wulfften-Palthe .... NL

The actresses in 2019

Martha J. Baker
Nada Farhat
Lydia Merell
Heidi Meinzolt
Sabine Bollenbach
Valery Bossmann-Quarshie
Lesly Orr
Jenny Engelow
Giovanna Pagani
Andrea Marikovsky
Janette McLeod
Dr.Kristina Kargel
Lena Pieber
Adelheid Schmidt-Thomé
Greta Noordenbos
Dunja Khalil
Margarethe Tingstad
Helen Kay
Brigitte Castigneul
Kerry Mac Govern
Irmgard Hofer
Jane Grant
Laura Huonker
Mans van Zandbergen
Ali Ronan
Maki Kimura
Shahina Jeffer
Diana Hrytsyshyna
Brigitte Obermayer
Eva Maria Volland
Ingrid Sharp
Amy Todd
Ros Cook
Nike Wentholt

LEARNING
FROM THE PAST,
GETTING INSPIRED
BY THE PRESENT

AND BE VISIONARY
FOR THE FUTURE

Workshops at the Zurich Congress 2019,
presented by young participants.

1. RECLAIMING THE UNITED NATIONS AS PEACE ORGANISATION

Convenor: Andreas Zumach, Journalist

Challenges:

The reality of the UNITED NATIONS/UN is far from its Charta: "one country – one vote" (veto rights in the Security Council). The UN are involved more and more in geostrategic power politics. The R2P (right to protect) is used to justify interventions…

To Do's:

- Abolition of the permanent members and inclusion of other countries to the UNSC
- Feminize the UNSC, integrating gender perspectives
- Increase the level of participation of CSOs in all the bodies and conferences of the UN
- Relocate the UN headquarters to make it more accessible for the non-EU-citizens
- Strengthen Global education, critical thinking and more peace studies

2. GENDER JUSTICE AND DIVERSITY TODAY

Convenor: Helena Trachsel, Head of the Equal Opportunities Office of the Canton of Zurich

Challenges:

Diversity needs visibility and a transformative approach in the society. The big Horizon of Fundamental Change must be realised in small steps:

To Do's:

- Courage to speak up, to call out injustice when you see it!
- Compassion to support each other, to celebrate how far we have come!
- Mentoring to build networks of change, to help young women see the difference we can make
- Collective to organise international summer schools and international exchanges on issues pertaining to women and peace work

3. DISARMAMENT AND EUROPEAN INITIATIVES

Convenors: Giovanna Pagani, WILPF Italy; Irmgard Hofer, WILPF Germany

Challenges:

Increasing armament and arms transfer, threats by weapons of mass-destruction (WMD), small arms and light weapons (SALW).

To Do's:

- ban military culture and shift to education focused on peace culture
- promote nonviolent solutions, media for peace
- Dismantle NATO
- Strengthen the Women-Peace and Security Agenda /WPS
- End the war industry and corruption
- Move money: from war economy to peace
- Sign and ratify treaties (Nuclear Ban Treaty etc.)
- Support the World March for PEACE!

4. PEACE EDUCATION AND ENVIRON-MENTAL JUSTICE

Convenors: Virginie Poyetton, cfd – the Swiss feminist peace organisation; Margarethe Tingstad, environmental expert WILPF Norway

Challenges:

Climate change affecting the survival of humanity, environmental education linked to peace education not implemented.

To Do's:

- peace education connecting the importance of climate and environmental justice and opposing militarism;
- change the narrative using storytelling, humour, non-violent communication, arts, empathy, compassion, solidarity;
- support the law of ECOCIDE as the 5th crime against PEACE by recruiting conscientious protectors of the earth and support the treaty to prohibit nuclear weapons;
- share best practices with a positive vision for the future

5. WOMEN VOTE PEACE

Convenors: Heidi Meinzolt, WILPF Germany; Slawomira Walczewska, EfKa
Poland; Ketevan Bakradze, AHA Austria; Carmen Magallon, WILPF Spain

Challenges:

Voting is a complex social-political process; Votes and elections always
set the course for questions of diversity, gender, justice and peace.
Vote Women! Vote Feminists! Vote Peace! Use your voting rights!
Peace from a feminist perspective means a decent life in dignity and the
respect of real needs, democratic participation and inclusion, justice
and respect of diversity for all

To Do's:

- Question patriarchy and de-gendering by right-wing political
  tendencies
- Strengthen a feminist analysis of root causes of violence and war and
  militarised masculinities
- Restore knowledge on (voting) rights and empower women
- Strengthen women movements, strikes and parity in parliaments
- Build a feminist movement, networks and raise women's voices

6. PEACE MOVEMENTS LOOKING FORWARD
Round Table of Swiss and international Peace Organisations

IFOR-MIR: Barbara Jost, Monika Wicki, Agnes Hohl, Anne-Lise Nicolodi

Challenges:

Need of a transformative power and influence on political decision-making – Peace is a Human right

To Do's:

- Stop investments in the arms industry
- Stop production and export of weapons
- Increase transparency of institutional power and investments of banks
- Enforce peace education and peace research
- Feminize economy
- Make everything legally binding!

COLLECTION OF ARTICLES REFLECTING ZURICH CONGRESS 2019

The following articles

are written by partners of the European project "Women Vote Peace" and by participants in the Zurich Conference 2019.

Some are more focussed on the situation of feminist peace activism in their countries, linking remembrance to actual challenges:

> Carmen Magallón, Spain
>
> Nina Sankari, Poland
>
> Helena Nyberg, Switzerland
>
> Maki Kimura, UK
>
> Ite van Djik, Holland

Others shed a light on topics discussed in the workshops

a) **education, culture of peace, solidarity, visions for the future:**

> Heidi Meinzolt, Germany
>
> Andrea Marikovski, Hungary
>
> Ketevan Bakradze, Austria, Georgia
>
> Valentina Uspenskaya, Russia
>
> Irmgard Hofer, Germany
>
> Slawomira Walczewska, Poland

b) **disarmament:**

> Giovanna Pagani, Italy
>
> Liat Biron, Israel

c) **environmental justice and feminist economy:**

> Virginie Poyetton, Switzerland;
>
> Rosalyn Cook, UK
>
> Annemarie Sancar, Switzerland,
>
> Gulnara Shahinian, Armenia

"Perhaps", Helena Nyberg said in her farewell words,
"we will see each other again in 100 years – to celebrate peace"

FEMINIST PACIFIST WOMEN IN SPAIN AT THE BEGINNING OF THE 20TH CENTURY

By Carmen Magallón[1]

The international women's movement began its articulation in the late 19th and early 20th centuries by the creation of three organizations:

a) The International Council of Women (ICW), founded in 1888;

b) The International Woman Suffrage Alliance (IWSA), founded in 1904 and

c) The Women's International League for Peace and Freedom (WILPF), founded in 1915. According to Rupp, the relationship between these three organizations can be told as being like grandmother, mother and daughter, since each emerged from the previous one.[2]

At the beginning of the 20th century, the IWSA had managed to unite millions of women from a large number of countries, in an organized movement to achieve the right to vote and, in principle, also to favour peace. At that time, it was a commonplace to think of a feminine nature endowed with peaceful virtues. The suffragists used this belief to benefit their cause, arguing that when women voted the world would achieve a permanent peace. Although not all the voices that stand up for peace shared the idea of women as essential pacifists. In 1914, Bertha von Suttner, who in 1905 had received the Nobel Peace Prize, spoke in the following way to the Women's Movement for Peace in Germany:

> "Some people think that women are hostile to war by nature. They are in an error. Only progressive women, those who have been able to educate themselves in a social awareness, who have had the strength not to be fascinated by institutions with hundreds of years, also find the energy to oppose them".[3]

---

1   *WILPF Spain. President of SIP Foundation. This article contains excerpts of a book to be published soon: Sandra Blasco and Carmen Magallón, Una historia de WILPF en América Latina y España, Barcelona, Icaria.*

2   *Leila J. Rupp (1997) Worlds of Women. The Making of an International Women's Movement. Princeton, New Jersey: Princeton University Press, 1997.*

3   *Sybil Oldfield (1989) Women against the Iron Fist. Alternatives to Militarism, 1900-1989, Cambridge, Basil Blackwell, p. 210. Cited in Carmen Magallón, Mujeres en pie de paz, Madrid, Siglo XXI, 2006, p. 44.*

The debate on the female vote in relation to the achievement of peace in the world is a classic one. The essentialist views of human nature united women to peace; a link persistently maintained no matter that along history, when women had the suffrage, women did not always vote for peace: the essentialist idea was not corroborated. Said that, denying that women are more peaceful than men are, we have to add that this is not to diminish the women's great role as builders of peace: the most powerful and persistent movement for peace in history came out of organized women.

In the 20th century, the milestone that marked the beginning of a pacifist feminism happened in the International Congress of Women, held in 1915 in The Hague, where an important number of suffragists met and proposed twenty resolutions for eradicate war. The proposals and sprit of that event became the philosophical foundations of the League of Nations, precedent of the United Nations (UN). For their contributions, the women of that congress are considered the remote mothers of the UN. Within that congress was born the International Committee of Women for a Permanent Peace (WILPF first name), the oldest and most lasting (still working nowadays) organization of women for peace in the world.

In Spain, a country which was involved in continuous wars (USA, Cuba, Morocco…), some women organized against the slaughter of their sons in those colonial and internal fights. The first pacifist initiatives of Spanish women took place within the campaigns against the war of Cuba-USA in 1898 and against the sending of soldiers to Africa in 1909. Women organized protest demonstrations, collective actions against the war and against the regime. Mothers of potential soldiers had a special role: they broke into the public sphere and showed their opposition to the political, economic and social decisions of the moment. They combined the defence of life with claiming access to political rights and citizenship. Women with secularists and internationalist ideas gathered their hopes in pacifism and envisioned suffrage as a necessary horizon to improve their lives. In the words of Dolores Ramos,

> "Women took to the streets spontaneously to defend the right to life of their children [...] but in doing so they not only broke into the public sphere but also elaborated their own policy and prioritized peace as a supreme value full of ethical content".[4]

---

4   *María Dolores Ramos (2008) "Republicanas en pie de paz. La sustitución de las armas por la justicia, el arbitraje y el derecho (1868-1899)", Pasado y memoria. Revista de Historia Contemporánea, 7, Madrid, 35-57, p. 49.*

The freethinking pacifist women in Spain were internationalist and aware of what was happening outside their borders. Although most of them could not afford to travel for attending congresses around the world, they followed the feminist debates and claims showing their adhesion through letters, statements and articles published in their magazines. They knew how feminists organized abroad and agreed to the need for women's union regardless of their ideology and social class, if they wanted to advance their rights. In 1902, they welcomed the Universal Congress of Freethinkers in Geneva[5] and in the early 1920s, on behalf of the Society 'Concepción Arenal' they would enthusiastically join the resolutions adopted by the WILPF congress in Zurich. Their stance as women, who did not wait to obtain rights to use them, placed these women close to international pacifist organization, whose practices followed this pattern.

The first Spanish feminist organizations grew up in Valencia founded by enlightened women who enrolled within the tradition of secularism and freethinking. The Valencians had friends in different cities (Madrid, Barcelona…) of the country, among other Angeles López de Ayala who directed in Barcelona 'La Sociedad Progresiva Femenina', whose objectives were to promote the secularization of customs and contribute to an education of women in civic values. Catalan freethinker women shared ideas and maintained close ties with those of Valencia. These women positioned themselves against those who identified war and patriotism with politics and against those who justified the need to die and kill human beings of flesh and blood for the sake of defending an abstract homeland. Belén de Sárraga was one outstanding leader of that movement. She was a freethinking teacher linked to Freemasonry and Spiritualism who took her ideals to different countries in Latin America. The press mistreated her and the regime persecuted and imprisoned her several times. The former led her to live in Uruguay and Chile, countries where she became a recognized and admired figure. Belén defended universal democracy and identified the struggle for female emancipation with the pacifist cause.

---

5   Ramos, Dolores y Vera, M. T. (1998), "El Congreso Universal de Librepensadores de Ginebra (1902): una aportación a la historia del pensamiento igualitario", Baética, 20, Málaga.

The following excerpt is a sample of her pacifist ideas:

> Is it a crime not to love borders? I declare myself a criminal. Is it a crime to hate weapons of destruction? I am a criminal. For me, what means instrument of death is abhorrent; both the dynamite and the scaffold, the cannon and the dagger. Nature, mother and creator is the only one who has the right to life and death; man unable to create life has no right to destroy it.[6]

These precedents are the prelude to pacifist feminism in Spain and the reception of the ideals that marked the insertion of WILPF in our country.

Women's suffrage in Spain

Clara Campoamor

In Spain, feminine suffrage came later than in other European countries. It is noteworthy that two women defended opposing positions in the Spanish Parliament: Clara Campoamor stood in favour of women's suffrage and Margarita Nelken against. The reason why Nelken and her political party opposed feminine suffrage was the fear that the influence exerted by catholic priests on women would push them to vote conservative parties. Finally, Clara Campoamor won the debate. Spain's women ought her the right to vote achieved in 1931.

With regard to WILPF, Spanish women knew their birth in the Hague Congress. The journalist María Lejárraga informed about the event and soon after the existent feminist organizations in Spain stablished links. Those years, the feminist pacifist journal 'Redención' served as a way Spanish women to keep in touch with international feminism. The sisters Ana y Amalia Carvia Bernal had founded this journal in Valencia in 1915, the same year they also founded the feminist Society 'Concepción Arenal'.

In its number 1, 'Redención' dedicated four of its fifteen pages to talk about peace and to publicize a circular sent by a recent created associati-

---

6   *La conciencia libre, 27 de junio de 1906. Cited in Ramos, María Dolores, Op. Cit., p. 54. My translation.*

on in Geneva, to which some of 'Redención' editors had already joined: The 'Union Mondiale de la Femme pour la Concorde Internationale'. The publishing group relied on universal principles of solidarity and mutual recognition, disseminated information on the rights achieved by women in Europe and other countries of the world, especially in Latin America, and joined them in their commitment to peace, suffrage and female instruction.

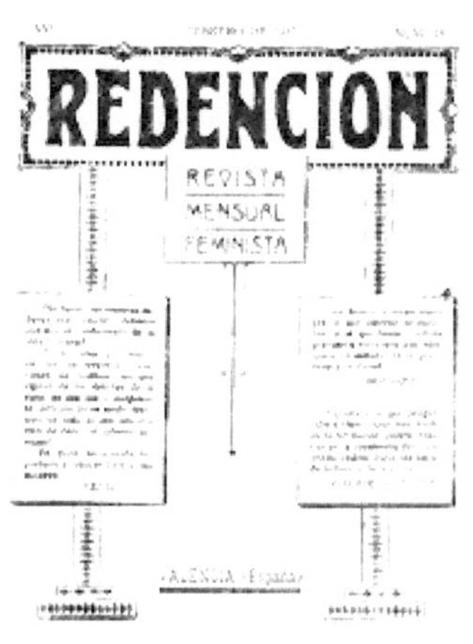

In fact, the magazine 'Redención 'was an exchange channel that connected Spanish women to some Latin American feminist organizations: with the Uruguayan National Council of Women, a member of the ICW that published Acción Femenina. The magazine contacted also to the Mexican Feminist Council through the exchange with its publication La Mujer Moderna and with the suffragists of the International Woman Suffrage Alliance (IWSA). It was one of the first Spanish publications to defend the feminine suffrage. The rapprochement and connection among feminist magazines was important to build a pacifist feminist internationalism.

In April 1918, the women of 'Redención' and those of the Society 'Concepción Arenal', with the support of the 'Madame Stael' Society of Pontevedra, and 'La Sociedad Progresiva Femenina' and 'La Mujer del Porvenir', both from Barcelona, launched a manifesto that was signed by fifty-four women from different Spanish cities. Based in it all together founded La Liga Española para la Progreso de la Mujer (LEPM), with Ana Carvia as its president and Amalia Carvia, secretary. The LEPM was the first feminist pacifist organization in Spain and the first to send to Parliament a request on women's vote. It responded to the desire to coordinate the different feminist groups of the country in order to get the right to suffrage[7]. It would also follow in the footsteps of the Concepción Arenal Society in terms of international connections. Like the latter, the LEPM established relations with Uruguayans, Mexican, and the IWSA, contact which led to Spain appearing for the first time in a section of the international suffragii magazine, Jus Suffragii:

7   Concha Fagoaga (1999) La herencia laicista del movimiento sufragista en España, en Ana
     Maria Aguado (aut.) Las mujeres entre la historia y la sociedad contemporánea, Valencia,
     Generalitat Valenciana, 29-112, p. 107.

Spain: We are pleased to receive copies of the Feminist paper, Redención. It appears from the September issue that it has now completed its third year of publication. In its first year, it founded the women's group Concepción Arenal, and helped to establish a library. Later on, it helped to constitute the Spanish League for the Progress of Women. It calls on all women to cooperate in working for their rights.[8]

The IWSA wanted to hold its first congress after the Great War in Spain, which had been a neutral country. For this purpose, at the end of 1919, the international organization sent to Madrid the Scottish Chrystal Macmillan[9] IWSA's secretariat and WILPF cofounder. In Madrid Macmillan met with the recently organized Spanish feminists. All of them agreed that María Lejárraga would be the person in charge of the Spanish organization committee. Nevertheless, all efforts were in vain. Tensions and conflicts emerged among Spain feminist leaders and the IWSA congress proposal thwarted: eventually the congress was held in Geneva.[10]

The 'Concepción Arenal' Society and WILPF

The women of the Concepción Arenal Society, through their contacts with IWSA, knew of the WILPF congresses and the resolutions adopted at them. As the original trunk from which they had emerged, WILPF leaders also belonged to the IWSA. Because of these overlaps and interrelationships, it is not strange for the Concepción Arenal to connect with WILPF and to be the first Spanish organization that appeared in one of its reports.

In those years, WILPF was not a very structured organization rather a standing committee that was taking shape at successive congresses. At the one held in Vienna in 1921, WILPF amended its Constitution: from now on delegates attending its congresses will have to be members of a national section, that of the country they represent, which suggests that it was not so before.[11] Regarding 'official' membership to the organization, in Secretary-General Emily G. Balch's report to this third congress (Vienna, 1921) she implied that maintaining ties through correspondence with a group, specifically referred to a group in Japan, was practically a membership.

---

8   *Jus Suffragii, noviembre 1918, p. 21. Cited in Aguilera Sastre, Juan e Isabel Lizarraga Vizcarra (2010) De Madrid a Ginebra. El feminismo español y el VIII Congreso de la Alianza Internacional para el Sufragio de la Mujer, Barcelona, Icaria, p. 116.*
9   *On Chrystal Macmillan see Helen Kay biographical note: https://womenvotepeace.com/women/chrystal-macmillan-bio/*
10 *Aguilera & Lizarraga, Op. Cit.*
11 *WILPF, Report of the Third Congress, Vienna, 1921, p. 299.*

> This group is not ready to go so far as our programme calls for and does not propose to ask, at any rate at present to join us as a Section. It will however remain in contact with us by correspondence, which in practice may amount to much the same thing.[12]

This commentary serves to contextualize the letter sent by the Society Concepción Arenal to the WILPF Congress in Vienna, a letter referring to the Zurich congress.

> The Society "Arenal", Barcelona, wrote accepting with enthusiasm the resolutions adopted by the Congress (at Zurich) which expressed their aspirations as well as those of the whole feminist movement. In Valencia, Barcelona and Madrid, which are the centres of Spanish feminism, the society is zealously working to reform the laws that depress the condition of the women of Spain, and to obtain the vote. In working for universal peace they wish to give an example of the civic virtues, to promote the welfare of the Women's International League and to secure universal disarmament.[13]

Did this letter, supporting the resolutions adopted two years earlier, in 1919, at the Zurich Congress, just the first WILPF held after the end of the war, did not mean a desire for belonging?

In Zurich, the pacifists had criticized the resolutions that came out of the Covenant of Versailles, considering that the humiliation of the vanquished contained in it planted seeds of resentment that would one day germinate again in clashes. They had too decided that the International Committee on Women for Permanent Peace should become a League for Permanent Peace, adopting the name that has subsequently endured, WILPF. The women of the Society Concepción Arenal shared the criticisms of the Covenant of Versailles and stood next to the pacifists of the League. In a harsh post-war context, WILPF's stance was difficult to maintain. That is why the expression of support had its importance. Spanish feminists hoped, for their part, that WILPF would be an aid in obtaining suffrage – which other European countries and the United States had just achieved – and for the amendment of laws that oppressed Spanish women and undermined universal peace.

Another Spanish organization showed its adherence to the agreements of

---

12 *WILPF, Report of the Third Congress, Vienna, 1921, p. 52.*
13 *WILPF, Report of the Third Congress, Vienna, 1921, pp. 155-156. Esta cita está también incluida en Aguilera y Lizárraga, 2010.*

LAS MUJERES ESPAÑOLAS Y EL PACIFISMO

La Federación Internacional Femenina de España, que días atrás inauguró brillantemente su labor pública organizando la conferencia que dió el Sr. Francos Rodríguez en el local de la Academia de Jurisprudencia, acaba de dar otra muestra de vitalidad enviando á la presidenta del Congreso Femenino de Zurich el siguiente radiograma:

«La Federación Internacional Femenina de España se adhiere con entusiasmo á los acuerdos del Congreso feminista de Zurich sobre el resto. Madrid, domicilio social, Caños, 3.»

Sabido es que estos acuerdos sobre problemas internacionales, á que se adhiere la Federación de mujeres españolas, consisten principalmente en pedir que se terminen las guerras mediante una paz de reconciliación, no de odios, que pueda ser simiente de guerras futuras, y que no se constituya la Liga de Naciones según el plan imperialista elaborado en Versalles.

the Zurich Congress, the Federación Internacional Femenina de España, founded and chaired by Celsia Regis (Consuelo González Ramos). The newspaper La Correspondencia de España echoed the sending by this Federation of a radiogram to the president of the feminist congress in Zurich. The radiogram explained her agreement with the "call for the end of wars through a peace of reconciliation not of hate, that can be seed of future wars, and that the League of Nations be not constituted according to the imperialist plan drawn up at Versailles."[14]

Conclusion:

At the beginning of the 20th century Spanish pacifist feminist were not in the central scene of the international women's movement for peace and freedom. Nevertheless, they were keeping in touch with the movement, they felt part of it and pushed and conquered important women's rights that contributed to improve their life… At least, until the Civil War (1936-1939) exploded.

---

14   *"Las mujeres españolas y el pacifismo", La Correspondencia de España, 19 de mayo de 1919.*

POLAND: WAR ON WOMEN

By Nina Sankari, Fundacja im. Kazimierza Łyszczyńskiego

Shadowed celebration

In November 2018 Polish women celebrated the centennial of their voting rights gained together with the restoration of the independence of Poland at the end of the World War I. However, it wasn't just a historical coincidence but a result of a long and tough fight of Polish women for their rights. But do the Polish women have really a reason for jubilation today?

One hundred years later we face an open war against women in Poland. It should be taken both as a warning and a call for women's mobilization internationally. Nearly 90 years after the Polish women obtained the legalization of abortion for medical reasons or rape in the interwar period, the Polish Government wants to send them back to the days of partition. Total ban on abortion with criminalization of woman, abortion being considered without exception as a crime, which they propose repeatedly, is a law that had been in force under the partition of Poland. Today the Polish Government treats the female citizens as did the occupants more than one hundred years ago.

Paragraph can kill

Paragraph can kill, used to say **Tadeusz Boy-Żeleński**, the author of 'Hell of women' who struggled in the twenties of the past century against the total prohibition of abortion and the criminalization of women and for the legalization of abortion for social reasons.

In 1932, a law authorizing abortion for medical reasons, and in the case of pregnancy resulting from a "criminal sexual act" (rape, incest, any sexual act with a minor) was adopted in Poland. At that time, it was the most liberal legislation in Europe (except the Soviet Union).

The legalization of abortion for social reasons was allowed in Poland in 1956. Declaration of a woman about her difficult life situation became an sufficient reason for having a legal abortion. Maria Jaszczuk, rapporteur of the Bill, persuaded deputies to vote ''yes'' with figures: 300 000 illegal abortions carried out by the "angel makers'' per year, 80 000 women admitted to hospitals each year after a clandestine abortion, of which 2%

died. Thanks to this law, Polish woman have benefited from the right to free choice and self-determination for 36 years.

Women back to hell

Now our patriotic Polish government wants to send them back to hell. With the new passports holding an inscription: God, Honor, Patria. 30 years after the democratic transition, women take the streets in defense of their fundamental rights and there are massive protests in defense of democracy. How is that possible?

The famous democratic transition of 1989 in Poland was accompanied by the systematic appropriation of power by the Catholic Church through its alliance with the conservative right. The Catholic Church presented a heavy bill for its role in the downfall of the so-called communist regime. And that bill was and continues to be paid in a currency called "women's rights". The Polish episcopate erased the principles of separation of Church and State, of secularism or neutrality from the new Constitution.

Polish women have paid this change with their health, their lives and the loss of their bodily autonomy. Under the pressure of the Catholic Church a very restrictive anti-abortion law passed in 1993. A million and a half signatures calling for a referendum on the issue were simply overlooked. The reproductive and sexual rights of women have become the war booty for the Church and its political partner – the right wing. In 1993, a very restrictive anti-abortion law (legal only in the case of danger to the health and life of women, serious malformations of the fetus and if the pregnancy is the result of a criminal act) was passed in violation of the fundamental principles of democracy. The current law referred hypocritically to as a "compromise" (concluded not with women but with bishops) allows in theory a legal abortion in these situations but practice shows that once free abortion is banned, even legal cases of abortion are no more respected, causing untold suffering to women or children born with severe malformations.

Church and populist right alliance to the assault on democracy

This is how our democracy started: with loss of the right to self-determination of half of the population. Polish women became the third-class citizens: after the male and the unborn citizens. But what began with depriving women of their fundamental rights, now ends with the destruction of democracy, of civil liberties and human rights for all!

Poland "crucified" the parliament, nurseries, banks, post offices; public school converted to catholic madrasa, researchers who are under pressure to restrict the freedom of scientific research; artists with their mouth gagged; doctors and teachers encouraged to recognize the supremacy of the divine law over the state one, lawyers relying on the canon law, priests who are above the law and the deputies praying for rain or smelling the stench of satan while listening to the project bill on secular school. The Law and Justice government pushed the destruction further, eliminating the balance of legislative, executive and judiciary powers, ruining the Constitutional and Supreme Courts, etc.

The Catholic Church in Poland assembled all conditions to achieve its objective of an absolute power in Poland. Since the teaching of Polish bishops was not convincing enough, they must impose their injunctions and prohibitions by political force. The Polish episcopate issued yet another bill to be paid by the Polish Government, and it is denominated again in 'women's rights'. On spring 2016, catholic fundamentalists have presented a project bill of total ban on abortion and criminalization of women, medical staff and any person involved in abortion. This project, prepared by the organization "Ordo Iuris" in Amsterdam, collected 450,000 signatures and received support from the Polish Government. It was the most important women's rights infringement since the period of the interwar. It would condemn to death the woman for whom the pregnancy poses a threat. It requires also that woman carries to term the pregnancy with a non-viable fetus and then look, powerless, at the agony of the child.

Resistance

The condemnation of this barbaric project was able to mobilize not only feminists and secularists but all Democrats, including Christian circles who oppose Catholic fundamentalism and authoritarianism of the Law and Justice Party. Three former first ladies, the wives of former presidents, expressed themselves against this project in an open letter.

But the feminists wanted to break the so-called hypocritical 'compromise' on abortion, concluded over the heads of women. In 2016, the initiative of citizen's committee "Let's save women" proposed a project bill on liberalization of abortion law in Poland. It was an attempt to restore reproductive and sexual rights of women and men in Poland, rights to information, education preparing people to make conscious decisions in the sexual domain. The project included the possibility of legal and safe interruption of pregnancy up to the 12th week. It also included the proposal of publishing a list of physicians who invoke the conscience clause to reject abortion. The project has collected 250,000 signatures of citizens.

This bill was rejected at the first lecture by the Parliament dominated by the ruling Law and Justice party but the bill of total ban on abortion was sent to further proceeding.

This decision has provoked a real fury of women who had enough of being treated as incubators. The same day started "black protests", growing every day and ending with the biggest protest ever in Poland of the ,,democratic era". On 3 October, dobbed "Black Monday," thousands of women, wearing black as a sign of mourning for their rights, have gone on strike protesting the proposal of total ban on abortion. Polish women also boycotted the work, the universities and schools and refused domestic chores. In Warsaw, despite the rain, the city center was crowded with black protesters and the Castle Place was totally filled with women and men in black. Anti-abortion protests have been held around the country in 60 cities. The black protests of 2016 gave beginning to the mass women's movement – Polish Women on Strike which mobilized thousands of women not only in the big cities but in the small localities as well. The movement managed to organize another mass protest in Warsaw in 2018 to successfully oppose another government's attempt to further restrict the anti-abortion law. The representatives of the Polish Women's Strike run and obtained mandates in the local and European elections and now are numerous to be candidates for incoming parliamentary elections.

One of the claims of the Polish Women on Strike (OSK) was agreed unanimously as the first one at the beginning of its foundation congress. It was the claim for secular state.

Women's resistance proved to be a big force of mobilization. It is the biggest force actively opposing the rise of nationalism and fascism in Poland. It's clear that without liberation from religious oppression, there will be no women's rights, there will be no secularism not only in Poland. Without a secular state there will be no democracy. The populist right is using religion to establish an authoritarian state, whether it is an Iranian theocracy or European non-liberal governments that collaborate with fascist forces. The "illiberal democracy" invented by Orban in Hungary is not based on religious motivation, yet it has introduced the protection of the life from the conception to the Constitution.

In Ohio, women may soon be sentenced to death for abortion. Hand Maid Tale takes its place in the real life. Gilead is not only about women's rights, secularism and democracy. But oppression of women is the pillar of the patriarchy, the foundation of all autocratic systems and the enemy not only of women's emancipation. We are facing war on aspirations of humanity for emancipation in general.

War on women leads to the war tout court. We cannot allow it to happen again.

Black protest in Warsaw

WE WILL CONTINUE TO ADVOCATE FOR PERMANENT PEACE

By Helena Nyberg

Despite the fact that Switzerland is not a EU-member, history has shown that Swiss feminists have been connected to women in European countries right from the start of the Suffragette movement. Moreover, cities such as Zurich have played a particular role for the independent development of women in society since medieval times.

Brief Historical Background to the Feminist History of Zurich

As early as in 853 A.C., Zurich allowed the foundation of a Women's Monastery in Zurich, pre-empting the tradition of democratic structures allowing women basic rights, e.g. not having to marry, to be educated in public schools and to live together in communities (the Beguines). In 1247, women began to live together in beguinage houses and yards. They were socially active, earned their living and led a Christian-spiritual life without monastic hierarchy and vows. Many wealthy women donated their wealth to enable the foundation of a house in which women lived and worked together – including children and poor women who had left the country-side. Reformation was another milestone for women's rights: When Ulrich Zwingli (1484-1531) became pastor of the Grossmünster (1522), he demo-cratized life in the city and started to preach ideas of independence of mind; he insisted on education for all, hence, women had to be literate, as well. Himself, he married a woman who left one of the Zurich female convents for him. Despite all female and male Bürger were members of the guilds all through medieval times, women were no longer tolerated within the guilds at the beginning of the 19th century. Only in 1989, exactly forty years ago in 2019, Zurich women started to assert their right in being included in the traditions of the still existing guilds. They formed the Fraumünster Society and for the last 20 years they have been allowed to participate as guests of another men's guild (the Constaffel Society) in the biggest city festival, the "Sächsilüüte". Every year, before joining the Parade, the members of the Fraumünster Society gather in the "Fraumünster"-Church (the Women's Abbey), the former Convent of Katharina von Zimmern, who was the last abbess and highest political figure of medieval Zurich. Together with the reformer Zwingli, Katharina opened schools for girls and taught them how to read and write as early as 1504. The Fraumünster Society honour the abbess by putting roses on her tomb recalling her peaceful surrendering of the city to Reformation by handing the keys of the City over to the citizen's Council in 1524, thus preventing war between the Catholics and the Reformers. The open-mindedness of Zurich towards women's education is still seen in the fact that apart from Paris, Zurich has allowed women to study at the University from the 19th century onwards; which attracted mostly Russian female students as of 1867, but also Rosa Luxemburg and Anita Augspurg[1] "was haben wir damals die gemütlichen Herrenrunden mit unseren Diskussionen aufgemischt … mit unserem Schweizerischen Verein Frauenbildungsreform und dem internationalen Studentinnenverein haben wir den ersten Sturmlauf aufs Wahlrecht geplant …"

Our voting rights and commitments:

And notwithstanding that Switzerland being one of the last European countries to grant women the right to vote and be elected in 1971, Swiss feminists have shown a strong will to defend their rights and to advocate peace, even against the nationalist trends that prevailed between the First and the Second World War – a time when WILPF was not allowed to be active in "neutral" Switzerland. And following the celebrations of the 100th Anniversary of the 2nd International WILPF Congress in May 2019 in Zurich, women in Switzerland staged the 2nd national Women's Strike on 14th June, 2019, bringing together more than 150,000 women (and men) into the streets for equal rights and pay for women, migrants, People of Colour and LGBTQ as well as for visibility and compensation of women's unpaid (care) work. WILPF Switzerland participated with events for peace and disarmament. The outcome of "WomenVotePeace" will be taken up and discussed by WILPF Switzerland and Swiss Women's and Peace Organisations. It is unique in the political history of Switzerland, that the women came together representing the different political parties, trade unions, NGOs, Women's (peace) organisations, LGBT-groups from all ages and societal levels. The "Feminist Coordinating Collective" continues to cooperate, and calls for regular meetings to keep the momentum alive – and it has jointly been decided to call for another national Women's Strike in 2020! WILPF Switzerland members attend the meetings of the collective and are

1   from Anita Augspurg, Lida Gustava Heymann „Erlebtes und Erschautes"

advocating to mobilise for March 8, 2020, the International Day of Women. In 2019, the Swiss women's strike had to take place on June 14, because the first national Women's strike ever to be organised in the German, French and Italian part of the country took also place on June 14, 1991 – exact ten years after the Swiss law of equality between women and men had been passed, but not implemented to the satisfaction of the women. This is why they called for the 1st national Women's Strike on June 14, 1991. 28 years later, things have not much changed for women in Switzerland, but immediately after the strike in 2019, the national parliament passed a law for paternity leave of two weeks – at least. And women should be represented on Management Board of Directors, etc.

For 2020, WILPF Switzerland would like to benefit from the international structure of the oldest women's peace organisation represented in all continents to mobilise together with the women in Switzerland for another powerful expression of Feminist peace and commitment.

We have a right to peace – we will continue to advocate for permanent peace.

"The most radical thing we can demand in today's warlike world is peace," said Natasha Wey, President of the Women's section of the Social Democratic Party of Switzerland, in her welcoming address. "What enormous radicalism did the women around Clara Ragaz display in Zurich 100 years ago! How visionary were their demands and how courageous were their aspirations for a sustainable and peaceful world. This anniversary day should also be a prelude to the fact that women's demands will be taken to Swiss streets with the women's national strike in the international campaign "stop violence against women" and that women will intervene more strongly in politics – in Switzerland and in the world."

In Switzerland, since 2008, peace is also strongly advocated in the annual nation-wide campaign "16 Days Stop Violence against Women". The campaign was launched at international level in 1991 as "16 Days of Activism Against Gender Violence" by the Women's Global Leadership Institute. The two commemoration days of November 25 and December 10 were set as the start and end dates respectively. In 1981 Latin American feminists proclaimed the date of death of the three sisters Mirabel as the day of remembrance against violence against women. This was after the

Dominican secret service had the sisters murdered by order of the dictator Trujillo on November 25, 1960. The United Nations General Assembly has designated November 25 as the International Day for the Elimination of Violence Against Women. Human Rights Day on December 10 commemorates the year 1948, when the Universal Declaration of Human Rights was adopted by the UN General Assembly in New York. The two dates form a bridge from the south to the north, illustrating that violence against women occurs everywhere and is a global issue. On December 17, 1999, the date received its official United Nations (UN) resolution and has been taken up since by numerous women's organisations world wide.

In Switzerland, more than 60 women's groups and organisations celebrate the time from November 25 until the Human Rights Day on December 10 with various events ranging from theatre to film and discussion events, or street actions and exhibitions. Coordinated by the Feminist Peace Organisation cfd in Berne, women of all walks of life are free to join in planning and working our annual theme of the "16 Days" and mobilising during the summer months. In 2019, the theme is "Stop Violence against Women of Age" – violence can take various forms, such as structural, physical or mental violence exerted by institutions, strangers, care givers of family members.

WILPF Switzerland joins the campaign and cooperates with the Swiss Center for Information and Support in Case of Violence against Elderly Women. In the past, WILPF has cooperated with human rights organisations in support of indigenous women highlighting the rampant violence in countries such as Canada, Columbia, Ecuador and Honduras. In 2018, WILPF invited the Zurich "Mannebüro", the Support Center for men who seek advise, to join forces in an excellent event to explore the roots of machismo, power structures and violence against women.

REFLECTIONS ON COMMEMORATING WOMEN'S ACTIVISM OF THE EARLY 20TH CENTURY: SUFFRAGE, PEACE, TRANSNATIONALISM AND DIVERSITY

By Maki Kimura, WILPF UK

Abstract

Over the past few years, the First World War Centenary (2014-2018) and the celebration of women's 100 years of suffrage in some European countries in 1918 have provided a wealth of opportunities in Europe, in particular in the UK, to revisit and acknowledge the legacies of the First World War from different perspectives. In addition, it has represented an opportunity to review the history of women's activism in the late 19th and early 20th centuries. This series of events commemorating the past is, however, not simply a mechanism for rediscovering and recording the past, but represents a very political act of memorialisation – identifying what is worth remembering and selecting what to remember and how; a question strongly entangled with and influenced by the politics of today. For example, even with extended lists of events and studies undertaken during this period of celebration, what was often missing was coverage of the story of feminist pacifism in the early 20th century. The Women vote Peace Project funded largely by the Creative Europe Programme of the European Union (2018-19) is one of the few exceptions that has tried to bring this often-forgotten history of women's activism into the public domain. Drawing on the experience of being involved in the project commemorating activities and achievements of feminist pacifists of the early 20th century, this article sets out to reflect on challenges that the (feminist) act of remembering faces in this process of commemoration of the past.

Key words: memorialisation; women's suffrage; the First World War; feminist pacifists; transnationalism; diversity.

During the First World Centenary (2014-18) commemoration in the UK, there have been various events and projects organised in attempt to uncover and preserve diverse memories of the First World War. These involve those who fell, both soldiers and civilians including 'enemies'; forgotten heroes such as soldiers from the Commonwealth countries; the experience of women in war working as doctors, nurses and relief workers; and the lives of civilians at the home front. However, the narrative of those who objected to war was often absent, and the problem of militarism – the root cause of why so many had to suffer and lose their lives, as well as the fact that the war was fought in colonies in Africa and Asia, was largely obscured. In 2018, the UK welcomed another year of celebration – the 100 years of women's suffrage, though it should be emphasised that this did not apply to all women. Only those over 30 years with a property, married women whose husbands were householders or met a property qualification and university graduates were given the right to vote in 1918. Acknowledging the activism of courageous women of the early 20th century was a vivid reminder of the importance of inscribing women's history into mainstream history studies and a recognition of the gender inequality still suffered by many women even after a hundred years of women's suffrage.

However, in the commemoration of the 100 years of women's vote, voices of certain groups of women – working-class women, women of colour and women from the British Empire – were still largely marginalised. In the mainstream celebration, there was only limited acknowledgement of the contribution and differentiated experience of working-class women and women of colour in women's suffrage movements. Tens of thousands of working-class women did indeed join women's suffrage movements in Britain, linking the vote with other issues such as equal pay and better housing to improve living conditions. They endured harsher treatment once arrested, and the personal cost of the arrest was higher than for their middle-class counterparts. However, compared to Emmeline and Christabel Pankhurst, the names of another Pankhurst daughter Sylvia, who worked intensively with working-class women in East London, and of a working-class suffragette Annie Kenny are still not widely known. Similarly, while the suffragists/suffragettes in Britain were largely (middle-class) white women, women from colonies within the British Empire such as India, Australia, New Zealand, South Africa and the West Indies, were present at an empire pageant organised by suffrage societies in June 1911 to demand the right to vote at the coronation of King George V. The presence and the contribution of these women of colour in women's suffrage movements in

Britain, as well as how some of these women – such as those who had connections with India – became active in developing transnational networks and addressed issues concerning the right to vote, women's rights and independence, has now been acknowledged. However, what women's suffrage and other women's rights meant to women living in colonies within the British Empire was not widely discussed during the 100-year celebration.

What is most noticeable, however, is that the tribute to women's suffrage movements was strangely and overtly silent about the relation between women's suffrage (movements) and the First World War, though the celebration took place during the First World War Centenary commemoration. One of the few exceptions was the unveiling of the statue of Millicent Fawcett in the Parliament Square in April 2018. This was often reported (rather awkwardly in some cases) in the context of women's support for the war in their role as nurses and doctors as well as munition factory workers emphasising how this had led many politicians to champion women's enfranchisement. However, linking women's war effort and women's suffrage can be slightly problematic, as, first, while the First World War might have opened various opportunities for women, it was women's continuous struggle since the 19th century which helped them eventually to win the suffrage. Second, it overshadows the history of feminist pacifists of the early 20th century, who opposed the First World War and were themselves suffragists. The Women Vote Peace project, thus, played an important role in connecting the history of women's suffrage movements and the issue of war and peace at the same time providing an opportunity to examine how far we have progressed on the achievement of gender equality and peace since, and if not, why.

Women's suffrage movements started during the first half of the 19th century. However, it is well known that the movements only gained their full strength in Britain after reorganisation of suffrage societies under the National Union of Women's Suffrage Societies (NUWSS) in 1887, and once Millicent Fawcett (1847- 1929) became the president (from 1879 until 1919). The Women's Social and Political Union (WSPU) founded in 1903, led by Emmeline Pankhurst (1858-1928) and her daughter Christabel (1880-1958), had recourse to more militant acts to attract attention and those members were called suffragettes. It is worth noting that women's suffrage movements developed around the time of imperialism in Britain being intensified. In 1899, a humanitarian pacifist, Emily Hobhouse (1860-1926), daughter of a deceased archdeacon in Cornwall, was appointed secretary of the South African Conciliation Committee, a group that opposed the British government policy on South Africa. She made a trip to South Africa in December 1900, during the Anglo Boer War, and visited concentration camps producing a report on the condition of camps, which severely criticised British authorities' negligence. Her campaign caused a divide in the NUWSS in 1900-1901 – some members, including Fawcett, taking a more imperialist and anti-Boer stance, while others' allegiance was more pro-Boer. A looming war in the 1910s created further divisions between the suffragists and suffragettes in Britain and in other countries as well as among international suffragists. Fawcett and Pankhurst, the main figureheads of women's suffrage movements both in Britain and internationally, supported the war suspending their activities to prove that women are useful in mobilising the masses and helping the war cause. Some suffragist/suffragette women who were against the war, such as Chrystal Macmillan (1872-1937), Kathleen Courtney (1978-1974) and Catherine Marshall (1980-62) left the NUWSS to attend the first international congress of women in the Hague in 1915 to discuss war and peace, as the NUWSS did not support the congress declining to send representatives. This is how the Women's International League for Peace and Freedom (WILPF) started, though in 1915, it was originally called the International Committee of Women for Permanent Peace and the name WILPF was only adopted at the 1919 Congress in Zurich.

As is apparent in the way that WILPF was founded, 'not all suffragists were pacifists.' However, it is also important to recognise that, 'not all pacifists were suffragists' either. The tension between peace or women's rights (suffrage) – that is, which to prioritise – is exemplified by heated international exchanges in 1898 and 1899 between Bertha von Suttner (1843–1914), Austrian-Bohemian Pacifist and Novelist, who would later in 1905 be awarded the Nobel Peace Prize, and Dr Aletta Jacob (1854–1929), Dutch Physician and suffragist, who formed the International Women's Suffrage Alliance (IWSA) in 1904. However, in the 1915 Congress in the Hague, called by Dr Jacob, where over 1,100 women from 12 countries participated, attendants had to agree to two principles:

1. That international disputes should be settled by peaceful means.
2. That the parliamentary franchise should be extended to women.

Therefore, from its inception, the WILPF was unique in its core mission of combining peace and women's rights (suffrage) and actively promoting both. In 1919, women from 15 countries met again in Zurich after the First World War, scarred by the war and dissatisfied and frustrated by the on-going post-war negotiations.

Being involved in the Women Vote Project in re/constructing the narrative of the 1919 Congress in Zurich, I was keen on creating a space in this project to address the issue of diversity of women and intersectionality of this transnational women's peace activism of the early 20th century (or lack of it) and to what extent these women were aware of the issue of imperialism and colonialism. The First World War was not only fought in Europe, but was also played out in Africa and Asia, as it was very much a war in and over colonies – a fact which often remains overlooked today. Women's peace activism in the early 20th century around the WILPF was highly transnational, as it was developed on already well-established international networks of suffragists like the International Women's Suffrage Alliance (IWSA) founded in 1904. In addition, conscious of the lack of presence of Asian women in the 1915 Hague Congress, Macmillan subsequently wrote to a well-known educationalist in Japan, Naruse Jinzo who had founded the Japan Women's College in 1901, encouraging him to send delegates from Japan to the next Congress. While there were no participants from Japan in the 1919 Zurich Congress, the Women's Peace Association was founded in 1921 in Japan, which started to send delegates to the Congress from the one taking place in Vienna in 1921 onwards. Similarly, a WILPF group was in operation in British India from the 1920s. In the Report of the 1924 Congress in Washington, sections in Australia, Austria, Belgium, Bulgaria, Canada Czecho-Slovakia, Denmark, France, Germany, Great Britain, Greece, Haiti, Hungary, Ireland, Italy, Japan, the Netherland, New Zealand, Norway, Poland, Sweden, Switzerland, Ukraine, the USA were listed, and it also presents a record of receiving visitors and fraternal delegates from Bolivia, China, the Philippines, Cuba, Ecuador, India, Mexico, and Guatemala.

Transnationalism, however, does not necessarily mean that the women's peace movement was critical of imperialism and colonialism and effective at reflecting the diverse voices of women. A good example was Japan, which was an Asian country, but also was paradoxically an empire with colonies. Feminist pacifists then were not free from the values of the time either. For instance, 20 resolutions which were adopted at the 1915 Congress in the Hague were forward looking in emphasising the importance of the role of women in peace negotiation and general disarmament, but also referring to certain cultures as 'primitive people'. Although the extensive transnational nature of women's peace movement should be adequately praised, the celebration of transnationalism often masks such problems. We cannot rewrite history simply to make it more acceptable to us in the 21st century. In this commemoration project of the 1919 Congress in the Congress, I hoped for us to capture at least the history of our foremothers from the critical perspectives of the 21st century. Neither Indian nor Japanese women could participate in the Zurich Congress, but, as we see in the Return of the Dangerous Women film, a black American delegate – Mary Church Terrell – made a moving speech on the relationship between colonialism, racism and war. During the Congress, she tried to convince her white American and European delegates to adopt resolutions on 'race equality' and 'self-determination of people and the military use of native populations of colonies' and the former topic was clearly included in the concluding resolution of the Congress.

Of course, a single contribution of Mary Church Terrell does not – or did not – make the transnational women's peace movements diverse, anti-colonial or anti-imperial. Indeed, her presence as the only woman of colour in the Congress was a stark reminder of the challenge and limitation of the movements. However, having her voice distinctly captured and some white women being played by non-white women in the film – reflecting the racial and ethnic diversities of 21st century Europe – would allow us the room to seriously think about and engage with these issues. Remembering the past is not only about the past, but also about the present. Consequently, we need to critically engage with the past – looking back through the analytical lenses of the present, raising our concerns not only about gender, but also over racial and other forms of inequality, the legacy of colonialism and ongoing geo-political exploitation. Unfortunately, a hundred years on, we are still pushing for the same requests such as gender equal participation at all levels of decision-making and universal disarmament, but I hope that studying the history of our foremothers would provide us with a great insight into ways that we could move our political demands forward.

THE ZURICH CONGRESS OF 1919 IN 2019: HIGH HOPES AND PRACTICAL IDEAS

By Ite van Dijk

After the disastrous First World War women came together in Zürich. Women that were active in the suffrage movement and women active in the peace movement joined to formulate their high hopes and practical demands. Women's rights were seen as essential for their fullest contribution to the community and for building up world peace. The congress established this with a list of women's rights like suffrage, equality in family laws, equal pay, equal education and equal opportunities. It be would possible to ban war. A League of Nations could prevent war and solve conflicts between nations or other groups of people without killing each other. But the congress concluded that the proposed covenant of the League of Nations omitted a series of important conditions, like guarantees for democratic decision processes and immediate reduction of armaments by all member states.

Women's suffrage that was on its way in many parts of the world at the time of the 1919 congress, has been a driving force for women's emancipation. But it took and takes time to gain respect and political power. Reaching peace is a permanent job will keep us busy. After WW I geopolitics, nationalism, racism, a financial crisis, poverty and insecurity brought the Second World War, undermining optimism about humanity and a peaceful world. Feminist goals and peace work require long term efforts.

Peace activism in which many women and women's organisations were involved in the first half of 20th century had been labeled by mainstream politicians, influencers and newspapers as foolish and naive. But when you realize how much resistance and mockery women of the first feminist wave striving for suffrage endured it is understandable that they were not too shy to take part in the peace movement and express their high hopes for a safer world. Feminists are born to challenge the established order and bring forward visions that can change the world.

After WW II the second feminist wave that was facilitated by women's suffrage, peace and growing prosperity put old and new necessary practical changes on the political agenda. Non-discrimination laws, improved access to education and labour, availibility of easier birth control methods, and childcare were demands of the women's movement to gain freedom and more political power. Today the results are showing. The power of women is growing. The mockery of women striving for independence, power and a better world is no longer commonplace, on the contrary. Gender equality is no longer a forgotten subject. The European Commission, the International Monetary Fund and the European Central Bank will be presided over by women pretty soon.

However, a lot of creativity will be required to stop today's nationalist movements that are not in favour of gender equality, multicultural societies and pluralism. Neo-liberalism and climate change threaten society and nature. A lot of work needs to be done to stop women's oppression and violence against women all over the world. We can not lean backwards. We should continue to formulate what individual freedom, inclusiveness, pluralism and social justice means and how these can promote a safer world for everyone.

Recently an established Dutch newspaper wrote on thre front page "New moral leaders are young, female and influential" referring to Malala Yousafzai, Greta Thunberg, Emma Gonzáles and some others[1]. The young women attract many followers with subjects such as education for girls, climate change, private gun ownership in the US, populist issues, social justice, protection of refugees and political opposition in Russia. Media show a lot of interest in these women.

In Zürich in 2019 women peace activists gathered to get inspired by the courageous women of 1919 and to formulate high hopes and practical ideas for today. So we talked about feminist politics and feminist peace studies, a culture of peace by peace education and peace minded media, ecocide as crime against peace, no military agenda for the European Union, arms trade and a strong campaign for the Nuclear Ban Treaty.

We face today narrow minded nationalism, scepticism about international cooperation, a new arms race, proliferation of weapons on a large scale and an increased danger of the use of nuclear weapons. Let us continue to express our high hopes and to bring forward our practical ideas.

---

1   *NRC Handelsblad 17 August 2019 page 1, 6 and 7*

WOMEN'S VOICES COULD HAVE CHANGED HISTORY?!
LET US INFLUENCE HISTORY/HER-STORY

By Heidi Meinzolt

"The feminist movement succeeded to renew a tradition of international solidarity,
but also transnational cooperation and coordination"
(Cinzia Arruzza, Italian philosopher)

In 1919, a delegation of six members of Women's International League for Peace and Freedom / WILPF with Jane Addams, Clara Ragaz, Rosa Genoni, Charlotte Despard, Chrystal Macmillan, Gabrièle Duchêne stood in Versailles in front of closed doors. What was in their luggage from the congress in Zurich for the negotiating men from victorious countries to avoid future wars?

- universal disarmament
- peace education and social justice
- equality in all decision making bodies, including the League of Nations, as arbitral tribunal for preventing national unilateralism in politics in the future

Today, in a globalized world, the requests and activities of the feminist pacifist movement are on the same ground, but diversified. Local women are moving global and back to make it a success story.

Some examples: WILPF is "reclaiming the United Nations as a peace organisation[1] "and writing agendas for a Feminist Security Council[2]. Disarmament conferences around the world call for the ratification of the Nuclear Non-Proliferation Treaty, for restrictive arms export laws (ATT)[3], and a ban on the use of killer robots[4]. At the UN in Geneva, an alliance promotes

1   https://www.wilpf.org/it-is-time-to-rebel-it-is-time-to-reframe-it-is-time-to-resist-it-is-time-to-reclaim-the-un-said-the-participants-of-a-major-convening-that-gathered-together-women-led-civil-soci/
2   https://www.peacewomen.org/node/100653
3   http://www.reachingcriticalwill.org/resources/publications-and-research/research-projects/10637-gender-and-disarmament; http://www.reachingcriticalwill.org/resources/statements/14032-wilpf-statement-to-the-fifth-conference-of-states-parties-to-the-arms-trade-treaty-on-treaty-implementation
4   https://www.wilpf.org/wilpf-attends-meeting-of-experts-on-autonomous-weapons-and-14-states-call-for-a-preemptive-ban/

women's rights beyond the business case"[5] to ensure corporate accountability against gender-based abuse, to integrate intersectional feminist perspectives, to instore gender-sensitive justice and remedy mechanisms, to enable environments for women human rights defenders. WILPF addresses human rights violations under the Convention on the Elimination of Discrimination against Women (CEDAW)[6] and the Universal Human Rights Review Process (UPR)[7]. Local and national data and success stories reach relevant international commissions and are used for feedback nationally. In annual side events at the UN Commission on the Status of Women (CSW)[8], in FAO, UNESCO, UNEP, WILPF delegates propose solutions in NGO fora in the field of agriculture and nutrition, education and climate justice – all related to peace. At the climate summits (COPs), women from strong CS networks push their commitments for the Sustainable Development Goals/SDG[9]. In the civil society platform/CSP of OSCE[10], an international "working group on women and gender issues" intervenes on women human rights defenders, a gendered view on migration, shrinking space for civil society (not gender-neutral), on conflict prevention in a cross-dimensional approach. In (inter-) national committees and conferences, WILPFers work on NAPs to implement UN resolutions 1325ff to feature the 3 "P": **Prevention – Protection – Participation** to stop war and violence.

According to the broad range of ideas and activities, the question must be allowed: What could have changed in the course of history, if far-sightedness and demands of women, if "Her-story" would have played a significant role in peace processes up to now? The vision is to change mainstream narratives and develop a transformative power and agenda!

---

5   https://www.wilpf.org/portfolio-items/womens-rights-beyond-the-business-case-ensuring-corporate-accountability/

6   https://www.wilpf.org/cedaw-committee-recognises-extraterritorial-obligations-towards-human-rights-for-sweden/; https://www.wilpf.de/the-impact-of-germanys-arms-transfers-on-women/

7   https://www.wilpf.de/deutschland-im-upr-ueberpruefungsverfahren-des-un-menschen-rechtsrat/

8   www.peacewomen.org

9   https://www.peacewomen.org/wilpf_and_sdgs

10 www.civicsolidarity.org

STARTING WITH A GENDERED ANALYSIS
OF THE ROOT CAUSES OF WAR AND VIOLENCE

At the beginning of the 20th century, the pacifist women's rights activists drew their identity from the research of the root causes of war and violence. Their feminist critique of patriarchal structures, economic and power politics leading to war has a long tradition. We know the socialist women such as Clara Zetkin, Rosa Luxemburg, but also the radical bourgeois feminist movement with Anita Augspurg, Lida Gustava Heymann (just to name German examples). If we consider the continuity of structural discrimination and violence, their analysis is still relevant today. Women in 2019 experience that the current political focus is not on an "economy must serve the needs of the people and not those of profit and privileges"[11] and on freedom from fear and distress, but on neo-liberal capitalist policies of interest and power – cynically often described as serving "stability and security". When patriarchy feels threatened, politicians and parts of the society re-invent a bunch of so-called "traditional values", often in accordance with fundamentalist religious support, and send women back home. Women still request equality on the labor market, health care including reproductive health, equal access to resources, equal pay. Modern forms of exploitation, militarized masculinities, trafficking and slavery are threatening women's life and add to their (multi-) vulnerability. Women are the "social airbag" (Christa Wichterich) when the International community imposes austerity measures in crises that destroy social justice and necessary services. We know better: economic reforms have to integrate care economy, dismantle the dominant ideology of growth – only discussed in minoritarian circles yet and practice solidarity.

The lack of political will for adequate economic reforms has particularly dramatic consequences in a post-conflict period. A few examples: Privatization and liberalization for the "free market" in the Balkans have attracted foreign investors and guaranteed privileges for post-war elites. Many jobs got lost. Instead of a necessary conflict analysis, the population in Bosnia is now faced with a very fragile status quo, privileging ethnic elites[12] . Massmigration blocked in terrible situations on the Bosnian borders actually is adding to violence: "it is a humanitarian crisis, but it is more a crisis of

11 *L. G Heymann in the Hague 1915*
12 *See more: https://www.wilpf.org/portfolio_tags/women-organising-for-change/*

humanity – this one of the important feminist issue …"[13] In the Caucasian region, the IDP women's association "Consent" has been working on the rights of IDP women and girls[14] affected by the "frozen conflict" on the protection of rights empowerment and peacebuilding initiatives. In Armenia, the women's association "Democracy Today Armenia"[15] supports with success democratic processes, enhancing women's roles and invest in gender-sensitive and inclusive societies. The examples are numerous.

Women from the Global South put the fingers in the wounds of colonialism, neo-colonial trade structures, corruption and externalisation of problems from the North who still deals with authoritarian elites as a guarantee for stability. We should not forget what Maria Mies, the famous German feminist economist and sociologist stated that "neoliberal globalisation leads to war and, vice versa, wars promote globalisation"[16].

The "new" wars of the 21st century – even apparently local (Bosnia, Afghanistan, Iraq, Palestine) are global, never ending, if we don't turn around the logic in the 21st century. The neoliberal model of capitalist accumulation is itself in a deep system immanent crisis – not by accident. The survival of the planet is the top priority. It is no time for modest "reform agendas".[17] Alternative concepts, transformative agendas are more than needed. Women have many good ideas.

Why not implemented?

PARTICIPATION

In 1919, women had reached their voting rights in numerous countries (in Europe, America, Australia) and "men's politics had failed so substantially" (Anita Augsburg at the Zurich Congress after WW1). The clear will of the fore-mothers was not just to be counted statistically, but to count. actively use the suffrage to influence political opinion and to participate meaningfully on all levels of decision making as a voice for equality and peace.

Nevertheless, looking at the reality of women's representation in regional and national parliaments in recent times, we consider that we are farer from parity (50%) in 2019 than a few years ago (at least in Germany). The percentage of participation is even worse in peace talks (partly less than

13 Gorana Mlinare, Women for Change in Bosnia
14 „Through the eyes of women", Broschure from Consent, edited by. German MFA, Brot für
    die Welt, DRA, Civic Solidarity Platform
15 https://www.democracytoday.am/
16 M.Mies in Krieg ohne Grenzen
17 https://fridaysforfuture.de/

20%), although it has been proven in numerous studies that sustainable peace is only possible with women. The Beijing Platform for Action from 1995 and the UN Agenda on Women's Peace and Security provide clear recommendations how to strengthen women's participation. Nevertheless, the gender component in conflict solution is still largely under-estimated. As an example, the formal Bosnian peace process of the 90s took place completely without civilians, especially women's voices and experiences. Only the militarized ethno-national political elite was involved. Thus, as it happened also in Ukraine and Syria, those responsible for the war carry out the idea of „peace“. There were no war indemnities, especially not for women victims of SGBV. Social and economic inequality is greater than ever, cementing ethnic segregation. Quoting women of the region in 2019,“ our absolute priority for participation is avoiding harm and preventing next conflicts”. A promising method to reach these goals is since years practiced with women from Syria, Bosnia, Ukraine in feminist solidarity dialogues[18], exchanging about feminism and international law, the rebuilding of society, reconstruction, reparation. The knowledge of the local women and women's organizations on root causes of conflict, remedies and cross-border contacts should define their mandate to participate equally and on all levels of negotiations. Again: Neglecting women among decision-makers, inevitably creates new tensions, never-ending hostilities, traumata and stimulates continuous (often militarily supported) interventions in a vicious circle.

Why not implemented?

PROTECTION AND DISARMAMENT

"Women can never be protected in war and by weapons" (Lida Gustava Heymann 1915 in The Hague). Women can feel secure only if peace and freedom from fear are guaranteed. Instead, the business of fear flourishes[19] and there is a fatal connection between militarised masculinities and the use and proliferation of weapons. The challenge for women is to develop strategies to put an end to militarization in the minds and in technology. Universal disarmament – from small arms to weapons of mass destruction

18 https://www.wilpf.org/syria-bosnia-feminist-solidary-dialogue-2-0/
19 https://www.wilpf.org/six-months-after-the-global-study-from-a-politics-of-fear-to-solidarity-and-justice/

– drastic cuts in military budgets and redeployment of funds in line with the WILPF campaign "Move the Money from War to Peace"[20] therefore remain a top priority. Women are targeted by multiple forms of violence, a majority of instances stemming from the socio-cultural construct that defines status and roles based on gender. Consequently, most violent incidents occur behind closed doors and victims are silenced in the name of prudery and family honor.

With the concept of "Human Security"[21], the UN initiated a change of perspective: security as a complex phenomenon that considers poverty reduction, right to health, education, protection of natural resources and livelihoods. The concept was most welcome at least in the beginning by the feminist movement, as it reflected the complexity of "security" they had in mind. The concept was further developed in the Millennium Development Goals until 2010 and the Sustainable Development Agenda[22] / SDGs by 2030 where gender equality (goal 5) and peace and justice (goal 16) are explicit goals. Controversial remains with the feminists whether it would not be more appropriate, instead of "security" to focus on legal claims, as a right to healthy food, clean water, land rights, protection of property, equal participation, climate justice and peace.

At its congress in 2018, WILPF stated in a long tradition in a resolution on militarism: **"working to formally dismantle the industries that contribute to war and conflict, and negative environmental factors arising out of misplaced governmental priorities and contributing violations of human rights and degradation of the human condition…"**[23]. The Arms Trade Treaty/ATT where the WILPF project Reaching Critical Will together with members from Lebanon to Burkina Faso, Colombia and Germany are involved, has the potential to prevent gender-based violence under Art.7, which requires that state parties assess the risk of arm's transfers being used to "commit" or "facilitate" such violence. WILPF has published numerous resources to guide state parties for legal obligations. A lot of good ideas –
why not implemented?

20   https://www.peacewomen.org/WPS-Financing and Accra 2018 resolution on disarmament
21   UN Member States affirmed the universal value of human security in General Assembly resolution 66/290, adopted in 2012. In it, they agree "that human security is an approach to assist Member States in identifying and addressing widespread and cross-cutting challenges for the survival, livelihood and dignity of their people."
22   https://de.wikipedia.org/wiki/Ziele_f%C3%BCr_nachhaltige_Entwicklung#/media/Datei:Sustainable_Development_Goals.jpg
23   WILPF, Accra Resolution on Militarism

PREVENTION and CROSS-BORDER NETWORKS

At the beginning of the twentieth century, women in the international suffragist movement in Germany, England, France, and Russia warned about a coming war; they watched with great concern the rearmament, nationalist hate speeches and warmongering. They launched dramatic appeals to "the women of Europe" (L. G. Heymann) and governments. Nevertheless, they could not stop WWI. Immediately after the War they met, as agreed in The Hague in 1915, for reconciliation and the continuation of their political work, in Zurich in 1919. At that time, the feminist-pacifist movement was active and well connected especially in Europe and America. 100 years later in the globalized world, feminist networks exist across all continents. Thus, the 1st WILPF Congress in Africa took place in August 2018 in Accra/Ghana. Especially in Africa, women's peace groups grow and develop power and momentum to bring about a change.

A new generation of young women who engage on an academic level and in local struggles, play a vital role in peace-related activities. The "Fridays for Future" global movement combines climate justice with human rights and peace. They provide new impulses, concrete recommendations and visions for an urgent transformation and a sustainable future.

A bunch of new ideas envisioning the future was impressively demonstrated by the Zurich Congress in 2019[24] with participants from 22 countries from all continents who discussed in Workshops the UN-Reform, disarmament, environment and climate justice, violence against women, voting peace.

In history, international women's networks have repeatedly contrasted with the mainstream of nationalism and patriotism in their respective environment. Nevertheless, patriotism was also inherent in some women's organizations and pacifists were discredited as traitors, communists, Jews or Anti-Semites. The constitutional principle of "non-violence" in WILPF was challenged several times in history e.g. in the fight against fascism or in relation to revolutionary liberation movements. However, at the end, women always maintained contacts and exchange, even during the Cold War. 20 years after the fall of the Iron Curtain, women from the East and West together protest against new walls and borders, poverty, rollbacks. Cross-border struggles are a permanent

---

24 *https://womenvotepeace.com/zurich2019/*

learning experience, a great motivation and a real preventive force against excesses of racism and new nationalisms.

Today, one of the major challenges of international cooperation is dealing with migration, affected by environmental degradation, militarism, human rights violations, and misplaced governmental and corporate priorities, noting disproportionately gendered violence. "Migration affects women in a particular way. Committed to the maintenance of life around them, and the lives of human beings and nature, women, out of desperation, seeking a better life for their children, are forced to emigrate. A variety of fates await them, many of which are unfavourable. At the same time, women are leaders within the movements that defend land and human rights. We should invest in a culture of integrative dialogue, a climate of tolerance and welcome, and guaranteed human rights standards for the benefit of whole societies and their coherence"[25]. Women's networks stay for an asylum policy that allows legal escape routes, human welcome, prosecution of (sexualized) violence and specific protection for migrant women and children. A package of international solidarity, respect of diversity, diplomacy and awareness – the only way to avoid more clashes.

Why not implemented?

2020 ANNIVERSARIES FOR THE VOICES OF WOMEN

Anniversaries are due in 2020: Beijing +25, UNSCR 1325ff +20. They provide an opportunity to initiate new dynamics. When "Feminist Foreign Policy" (e.g. German Foreign Minister at the UNSC) is supplemented with "Feminist Trade Policy" (Swedish Minister of Economic Affairs) and the justice demands of the young Fridays for future activists, substantial progress has already been made in the minds.

We women, pacifists and feminists, are ready to face the challenges.

We vote Peace!

---

25   *2018 Accra WILPF congress resolution on migration*

WOMEN AS CHANGE AGENTS
THEN AND NOW 1919-2019

By Andrea Marikovszky

> *"The passion of the century is the real, but the real is antagonism.*
> *That is why the passion of the century – whether it be a question of empires, revolutions,*
> *the arts, the sciences, or private life – is nothing other than war.*
> *'What is the century?', the century asks itself.*
> *And it replies: 'The final struggle.'"* [1]

On the very day, when I arrived back to Budapest from Zürich, where we celebrated the brave pacifist women, among them a wonderful Hungarian feminist, Vilma Glücklich, and the 100th anniversary of the first WILPF conference, Viktor Orbán, the Hungarian Prime Minister and Donald Trump, the Prime Minister of the USA, the country which owns the most of nuclear weapons, met to sign a contract about selling weapons for 1 billion dollar to Hungary, which is more than 300 billion Hungarian forints.[2] Besides, it is really absurd to live in such times when prime ministers have legacy to buy and sell weapons like gangland figures, we must take into account that in Hungary according to the statistics, 38% of the families (3,3 million people) live below the minimum subsistence figure.[3] This means that the income of these families (most of them has more than three children, so it means poverty of the mothers, too!) is less than 90,450 HUF/month (about 300 euro). A billion dollar means a lot in such a country! So the Hungarian elite leaders do not seem to be interested in fighting against poverty, instead they decided to join politics – as we see in the history of the 20th century – always ready to start a new war.

To understand this act, we must see that the neoliberal capitalist era obviously was present in Hungary from the 80's.[4] The country was still suffering from the consequences of Stalinism and the Kádár era, exhausted by

---

1   original: La Siecle de Alain Badiou, edition du Seuil, 2005. https://palmermethode.files.wordpress.com/2018/11/alain-badiou-the-century.pdf on page 38.

2   https://168ora.hu/kulfold/milliardos-fegyver-es-gazvasarlasrol-targyalhat-orban-trumppal-de-az-amerikaiak-egy-kicsit-tobbet-akarnak-168062

3   https://merce.hu/2018/06/01/33-millio-magyar-el-a-letminimum-alatt/

4   https://merce.hu/2019/08/11/magyarorszag-az-allamkapitalizmustol-a-tekintelyelvu-neoliberalizmusig/

WW II, then by the cold war and by the Russian empire. The ones who took advantage in these times reappeared as a new elite since the 90's, and their main acts are to combine politics with market interest of the global capitalist bourgeoisie. So from one oppression of the so called socialist bourgeoisie, Hungary shifted to another oppression of the neoliberal capitalism. The left ideology of the oppressed has been distorted and demolished by the interest of this new-old elite which was completely supportive without any critics of the renewed economic-political ideas, which brought up "capitalist realism" [5], and sacrificed the country on the altar of profit maximization. These neoconservative-liberal politics demonize the state itself, make it ready to have all common goods being privatized or neglected (such as education and healtcare) and deify the entrepreneur and business man who can earn more than all the others. Such ideology based on market competitivness was just a new disguise for most of the people in Hungary of the well-known cold war situation. But now the rivalry is between the good denizens (who can earn money) and the bad ones (who can't). It meant for millions to fall back in even worse situations of insecurities, and to become immediately part of the underclass or the precariat, and this is especially true for women. Women have only one possibility for social mobilization: learning. This is how it is possible that in Hungary 39,6 % of women have higher degrees (26,4% of men), but the average payment of women doe not reach the two third of men's. It is also important to mention that Hungary has one of the highest rates in suicides and poverty. [6] The Hungarian elite offered the Hungarians as cheap labor force to the globalized multinational corporations, and let alone the rest, the ones who are not good enough for such work and give only miserable subsidies to them, almost not enough to survive. Especially jobs where women work are underpaid. So many of us necessarily take several jobs, or accept to be vulnerable, depending on male relatives and husbands. We have thousands of homeless people. Their officially uncounted number obviously grows from year to year. By now we have a registered law to push these people out from the city centers by the police, not to disturb the view of prestige investments and the elite or the tourist gaze.[7] As many other post-socialist countries, Hungary also can be found among the competitor states which strive for being chosen by the globalizing and financializing capitalists, so to earn the honor of being a

5   https://www.amazon.com/Capitalist-Realism-There-No-Alternative/dp/1846943175
6   https://dailynewshungary.com/hungary-has-the-third-highest-suicide-rate-in-the-eu/;
     https://bbj.hu/analysis/hungary-among-eu-countries-with-highest-poverty-rates_148538
7   https://books.google.hu/books/about/The_Tourist_Gaze.html?id=bhhtg1sz0YAC&redir_esc=y

capital dependent country. The Hungarian elite appears in the disguise of either neoconservative or liberal ideology, but both serve the same market oriented neoliberalism which keeps injustice and the sacrosanct property of tycoons, as all over the world. In such a system which has strong interest of having weaker ones existing in it, the support of the oppressed and the idea of cooperation, peace, and prosperity of all, had completely vanished from the political scene. The academic, cultural and art life or even social media take this role. All of them have little effect on real life. The "democracy show" is not a unique phenomenon as we know from Giorgio Agamben.

The geopolitics in 1919 (Versailles negotiations), created the still existing post-socialist territory. Hungary is at the very bottom of the international productivity chain and exposed to the loans of banks in many ways. As a consequence, a new labour and entrepreneurial migration started from Hungary to the western countries of Europe, where salaries are 10-20 times more for the same jobs. Parallel we are faced with "migration" of precariat, tourists and elderly people from the west to this "display window" country, which offers cheap food, flat, water supply, health care, nice girls, many women with high diplomas and extremely low wages. So we Hungarians started to name our country the pub & bedroom of Western Europe, where one can buy anything, as necessarily expected from a self-colonized country.[8] Also many Hungarian women have to get into the global chain of care[9], and go to work in western countries as underclass persons, nicely called maids, leaving their own families and children behind to even more poor women, or take part in the prostitution & pornography industry, which especially hits gypsy women. So it is really grotesque when our prime minister makes propaganda against migrant people in such a country, where we have about 1 million Hungarian people each year leaving the country as labour migrants.

All these problems bring up a lot of violence every day which effects specially women's life, who have historical disadvantages to men. The field of violence against women is the most addressed topic by Hungarian feminists. There are three civil groups assisting such women, but still we have data of around 140 women's death per year because of violence. So no wonder if among these social processes it is just another act that the authorial capitalist, Victor Orbán decides to buy weapons from Trump. It

---

8   *http://monumenttotransformation.org/atlas-of-transformation/html/s/self-colonization/the-self-colonizing-metaphor-alexander-kiossev.html*

9   *https://444.hu/2019/01/21/a-migracio-ami-magyar-csaladokat-tehet-tonkre-megis-alig-esik-szo-rola*

did not stir up the depressed society, it remained just another news in the media, followed by nothing else, but freaky silence.

So we have many in common with our foremothers of first wave feminism. We have so much fear, insecurity, and injustice[10], and so much to protect and appreciate. So we, pacifist feminists, who want to work for a better world, have to decide what to do with the system itself, which produces violence, war, exploitation, injustice, and becomes dangerous even to all spheres of life through uncontrolled carbon emissions and pollution.[11] This system does not want to give up using poisons, weapons, nuclear weapons, scientist research of technology for killing,[12] strong belief in competition, fight and victory of the ones who have already redundancy and privileges, so to keep on the sick image of patriarchal hierarchy. How can we change such a system, which has done so much to minimalize the autonomy of the subject to arrive to a post-political era and made people believe that "there is no alternative to neoliberalism"[13] and encourage them to allow the market principles to permeate all aspects of life?[14] We must very seriously seek for understanding what pacifist feminism really means today for our common future, to find the way for real change. Besides the depressing social crises, the shadow of the climate catastrophe also means a big pressure on all of us, which makes it obvious that we feministc all have to be eco-socialists if we want to be pacifists.

First we must make a statement: we do not want to be emancipated in such a system, because it would only mean assimilation but not the feminist future!

We must realize that in the time of repressive tolerance[15] the postmodern superego[16] of the post-political[17] epoch has been created. This individual does not realize the exploitation as exploitation and has no clear point of view about whether the war is good or bad, necessary or could be given

---

10   https://www.bertelsmann-stiftung.de/en/publications/publication/did/how-are-you-doing-europe/
11   https://www.lifeworth.com/deepadaptation.pdf
12   https://www.vox.com/2019/6/21/18691459/killer-robots-lethal-autonomous-weapons-ai-war
13   https://www.wikiwand.com/en/There_is_no_alternative
14   https://www.hse.ru/data/2013/01/28/1304836059/Standing.%20The_Precariat__The_New_Dangerous_Class__-Bloomsbury_USA(2011).pdf
15   https://www.marcuse.org/herbert/pubs/60spubs/1965MarcuseRepressiveToleranceEng1969edOcr.pdf
16   Žižek, Slavoj: 'You May!' Slavoj Žižek writes about the Post-Modern Superego. London Review of Books. 1999. March
17   https://www.youtube.com/watch?v=fh2cDKyFdyU

up for ever. No wonder that the will of male politics appears with the intention to push back women's social situation to the the time of the first wave feminism! This is expressed in the growing popularity, even among women, of such right-wing populist politicians as Trump, Orbán, Putin. Or it can be detected in the popularity of such a book published first in 2006 by Eric Zemmour, called the First sex[18], obviously eligible to the cultural logic of the late capitalism, and quarrelling with the Second sex by Simone de Beauvoir .

Today we must rethink the original goals and values. The first wave feminist movement belongs to the modern times and its creation and blooming is due to two main endeavors. On the one hand, the fight for women's voting rights, and on the other hand, women's deeply understandable will to become independent from the men's income: so women wanted to step into the labour market and become employees. In both of these endeavors, we can see the weakening of the sense for self-determination and social consciousness of women.

Today we must admit that we cannot have equality, in the frame of the existing capitalist form. So fight for equality also means to create new ideas of a coming post-capitalist society as women in Zurich did. And if we see the women's situation in this new image of post-capitalist society, we must give new notions to the work itself as the structural position of work against capital, which has a use in strengthening the power of civil society above the interest of capitalist economy. It also means we have to put strong emphasis on the unpaid social reproduction work of women which keeps the existing system going, and change the notion of work force as buyable goods and the aspects of life (even women's bodies) simply as objects for any kind of commodification. I would say: in a way we must start a new epoch where we live from trustfulness and image of the future and not from the money of the capitalism. We are also led to the field of a new society of post-work, where work means an ethical point of view and joy, not the exploitation of the weaker ones, the so called second sex, and the nature.

So put the question right: whether are we ready today as feminists to fight for real economic justice, post-work, and the universal basic income as a human right which can harmonize the societies of Europe. This even seems to be almost the opposite of first wave feminism when it wanted to

---

18 *https://en.wikipedia.org/wiki/Le_Premier_Sexe*

have women step into the field of labour and male politics 100 year ago? Do we want to fight for the right to create new social structural ideas for the future, or are we satisfied with reforming the existing system and make it more "feminism like", gender equal and keep on being supportive to lean in feminism? Can we admit – as Vilma Glücklich has said in 1919, Zürich – that the politics led by men have been discredited, a bankruptcy, because it unavoidably brings up competition, violence, crisis, social and ecological injustice and wars? Are we, pacifist feminists, able to give to the world a realistic social utopia opposed to the dystopia of the present male politics where selling and buying weapons by country leaders is not just tolerated but accepted? Can we carry on the women's act of Zürich conference to give clear notions and suggest policies to the society for the next necessary step under the growing shadow of the climate catastrophe?

Only through these questions we can overcome the passion for war of the 20th century. The pacifist feminism of the 21th century can find the way not towards the war, which will be the final one, but to a society which will be the first in history of modern times to war.

VORTEILE DER DIGITALEN GESELLSCHAFT & „WOMEN VOTE PEACE"

Ein Projekt als Digitalisierungsprozess der ‚weiblichen' Geschichte und Figuren, welche sie schrieben

THE OPPORTUNITIES OF DIGITAL SOCIETY & "WOMEN VOTE PEACE"

A project as a digitisation process of the 'female' story and those figures that wrote it

By Ketevan Bakradze

Abstract

The digitisation process nowadays does influence every aspect of our everyday life as members of the informational society. In 21st century information became main source of knowledge, furthermore the guarantee of gaining power almost in every respect. In the last couple of decades information is seen as more effective when it is digitally accessible. So did the project "Women vote Peace" digitise main information about important historical European female figures and the Congress in Zurich back in 1919 and by using this, it aims to facilitate the maintenance of the issues of women's rights and engagement for peace for the future generation. Herewith it should be noted, that the digital world does open broad spectre of opportunities for women in terms of networking and mobilisation, particularly in those countries, where the feminist discourses experience negative connotations and the voice of (ordinary) women are lost in silence.

Der Begriff Digitalisierung sowie damit verbundene Dienstleistungen und Prozesse haben im Zeitalter der Informationsgesellschaft[1] einen großen Stellenwert gewonnen. Der Produktion und Weitergabe von Informationen und dem daraus erworbenen Wissen wird in der Informationsgesellschaft große Bedeutung zugemessen. Heutzutage kann behauptet werden, dass ein großer Teil des Wissens von Informationen ausgeht und dementsprechend auf die Macht (in unterschiedlicher Hinsicht) zurückweist[2].

---

1   *Laut Duden ist die Informationsgesellschaft eine „Gesellschaft, die durch die Fülle der Informationsmöglichkeiten mithilfe der modernen Medien geprägt ist".*

2   *Referenz auf das Foucaultsche Konzept der "Archäologie des Wissens" und "Genealogie der Macht".*

Die Informationen bestehen nicht nur aus unterschiedlichen Inhalten und in verschiedenen Formen, sondern beinhalten zeitgleich auch politischen Charakter. Somit ist es nicht verwunderlich, dass der Bedarf an Digitalisierung und der damit verbundenen Transformation von (wertvollen) Informationen heutzutage zunehmend an Bedeutung gewinnt.

„Women vote Peace" ist ein internationales Projekt, welches den Anspruch stellt, eine Vielzahl von aus dem vergangenen Jahrhundert stammenden Informationen an die heutigen Standards anzupassen und für die nachkommenden Generationen die Suche nach Frauen, welche sich für ihre Rechte und den Frieden eingesetzt haben, leichter zu gestalten. Biografische Informationen über die Teilnehmerinnen des Züricher Kongresses im Jahr 1919 sowie das Transkript der Veranstaltung, welches sich mit relevanten Themen beschäftigt, sind bis heute auf Online-Plattformen nur mit sehr großem Einsatz und Aufwand zu finden. Infolgedessen existiert eine Notwendigkeit die Geschichtsschreibung mit weiblichen Aspekten, vor allem für heute aktuelle Themen, wiederzubeleben und einen Beitrag zur digitalen Archivierung dieser Zeit zu leisten, um somit in der Zukunft die Möglichkeit zu schaffen, dass die Relevanz zu diesem Friedensthema aufrechterhalten wird.

Im Rahmen des Projektes durchgeführte Aktivitäten wie die biografischen Recherchearbeiten über die historischen Figuren des Züricher Kongresses, die erfolgreich gelaunchte und stets in Bewegung befindliche Website des Projektes, die Veröffentlichung des Projektbüchleins in der digitalen und gedruckten Form sowie die Produktion des Filmes dienen wesentlich dem Transformationsprozess und hinterlassen dauerhaft Spuren in der Aktualität der Themen für die Zukunft.

Die Digitalisierung von Informationen zu den wichtigen historischen Frauen, welche den Frieden wählten, dafür kämpften, und von deren hervorgebrachten einflussreichen Fragestellungen, wird im Laufe der Zeit an Bedeutung gewinnen. Hierbei handelt es sich um eine nachhaltige und digitale Investition in die Zukunft, welche die Grundlage für kommende Generationen darstellt, um durch freien Zugang zu Informationen das digitale Wissen der Menschheit bereichern und weiterentwickeln zu können.

In diesem Zusammenhang muss eine andere Perspektive der digitalen Welt in Betracht gezogen werden, nämlich die Macht der digitalen Plattformen wie beispielsweise soziale Medien, welche einen breiten Raum für die (feministische) Vernetzung, vor allem auch in den Ländern anbieten können, wo Frauenrechte und feministische Diskurse größtenteils immer noch negativ besetzt sind.

Als gutes Beispiel dafür dient das Land Georgien, wo eine der bekannten sozialen Medien im Jahr 2016 eine Mobilisierungsplattform für aktivistisch motivierte Frauen bereitstellte. Vor drei Jahren sollen mehrere Frauen sich wegen der hohen Femizidrate (im Jahr 2015 registrierte 28 Fälle[3]; im Jahr 2016 unvollständig registrierte 21 Fälle[4]) hilflos und ziemlich zornig gefühlt haben. So mobilisierten sich zahlreiche Frauen auf der digitalen sozialen Plattform und überlegten die Wege zum Ausdruck ihres Protestes und zur Sensibilisierung der Frauenthemen[5]. Solcherweise wurde das Projekt „Women of Georgia" ins Leben gerufen. Das Projekt sammelt die Geschichten der Frauen und zielt mit deren Verbreitung auf die Inspiration und Stärkung anderer Frauen ab, welche ähnliche ‚unsichtbare‘ (Lebens) Geschichten teilen. Mithilfe der ‚unsichtbaren‘ Erzählungen wird das Bewusstsein über die Probleme der Frauen in Georgien geschärft, patriarchalische Kultur sowie deren Wirkung auf die Frauenlage in der Gesamtheit, sowohl für die weiblichen homogenen Gruppen als auch für die Untergruppen dargestellt und versucht tabuisierte Themen zu brechen.

Innerhalb kürzester Zeit gewann das digitale Projekt große Anerkennung und Interesse. Laut dem heutigen Stand weist das online Projekt auf einem der sozialen Medien knapp 70.000 Abonnent_innen auf und kann als eines der simpelsten und erfolgreichsten Projekte mit breiter Reichweite bezeichnet werden.

Werden die Vorteile der digitalen Kommunikation anhand des obengenannten Beispiels berücksichtigt, ist es bemerkenswert, dass diese sowohl als Mittel der Mobilisierung als auch zur nachhaltigen Strategie für Sensibilisierung der Frauenthemen dienen.

„… women must be given room for talking about their experience, particularly within the traditional, patriarchal society where you can hardly ever hear the voices of ordinary women."

---

3   http://www.parliament.ge/uploads/other/75/75684.pdf
4   http://ombudsman.ge/res/docs/2019041112492319382.pdf
5   Als Erinnerungsstütze und Referenz beziehe ich mich anbei auf die öffentliche Rede von Maia Chitaia in Wien im Frühling 2019, organisiert von der ‚Frauensolidarität‘ in der C3-Bibliothek für Entwicklungspolitik. Maia Chitaia ist eine der Mitgründerinnen des Projektes.

SEARCHING FOR PEACE: HOW CAN PEACE CULTURE BE IMPLEMENTED INTO EVERYDAY LIFE?

By Valentina Uspenskaya

> *We have but a partial civilization, heavily modified to sex – the male sex.*
> *Charlotte Perkins Gilman. Man-Made World. 1811*

> *"how can we answer your question, how to prevent war?*
> *The answer based upon our experience and*
> *our psychology—Why fight? — is not an answer of any value".*
> *Virginia Woolf Three Guineas. 1938*

In a world in unrest with a growing and rather generalized acceptance of militarization and use of force in international relations, it seems yet again of utmost importance to promote the vision of a culture of peace as "a necessary utopia" – to be reached in our time. I would like to begin my reflections for a culture of peace with a verse from a poem by the Swiss poet Conrad Ferdinand Mayer entitled "Peace on Earth" [1]:

But it is an eternal faith	Doch es ist ein ewiger Glaube,
that those who are weak and defenseless	Dass der Schwache nicht zum Raube
will not fall victim	Jeder frechen Mordgebärde
to any kind of murdering;	Werde fallen allezeit:
something like justice	Etwas wie Gerechtigkeit
weaves its way into and has an effect	Webt und wirkt in Mord und Grauen
on murdering and horror	
so that a realm will build itself	Und ein Reich will sich erbauen,
which will search for peace on earth .	Das den Frieden sucht der Erde

---

1   *Conrad Ferdinand Meyer. Gedichte. Ausgaben 1892, Hofenberg, 2015. S.140.*
A Christmas poem written by the Swiss poet Conrad Ferdinand Meyer (1825–1898) in 1886
and published by Austrian peace activist Bertha von Sutner (1841–1914) in her journal ‚Die
Waffen nieder!' (Lay Down your Arms! Also, the title of her1889 antiwar novel).

Searching for peace – this seems an appropriate formulation for what I believe peace culture means. In the following I pursue a question: **Searching for peace: How can peace culture be implemented into everyday life?**
It is paradoxical that when we speak of peace we do so in association with war and it is commonly perceived that to be prepared for war is the most effective means of reserving peace. There's an old military motto, "Si vis pacem, para bellum" from Flavius Vegetius Renatus circa 375 A.D: "If you want peace, prepare for war".

No, the world cannot be held by force. We must take another motto: If you would have peace, prepare for peace. If you want peace, prepare people for a peaceful life. A peaceful world needs peace-loving and peace-thinking people. Let the nations prepare for peace, by cultivating mutual goodwill, by the amicable settlement of disputes by arbitration, by agreeing to universal disarmament, by friendly cooperation instead of suspicious rivalry.

But there is no system of training for a culture of peace (in my country), there are no peace education courses in curricula, but everywhere there is military training; education of the young has focused on teaching them how to use rather than how to abhor the use of force. So, the culture of war remains dominant in today's society, in our schools, in the public and cultural sphere. As Russian progressive publicist and journalist Andrey Arhangelsky noted recently: "Patriotic films today take the form of an aesthetic admiration of violence and death per se. In a certain sense, this is a new stage in Russian cinema ... Violence in cinema is already breaking out of control, becoming self-sufficient and meaningful. This is probably the strangest tendency in Russian cinema of recent times – the death drive <....>"[2]

Here, I would like to touch only one issue of gender socialization: challenging man-gender norms. When discussing the possibilities of its formation, it is worth considering that almost half of the population are men on whom the dominant non-peace culture – the culture of war– practiced for centuries, exerts tremendous pressure, and which recreate this culture, including through TV, education and all the major social institutions under their control. The inextricable confusion of politics and warfare is part of the stumbling block in the minds of men. As Charlotte Perkins Gilman noted in the 1811: "Life, to the "male mind"... is a fight, and his ancient military institutions and processes keep up the delusion[3]: The 'hegemonic masculinity'

2   Abdrey Arhangelsky 14.08.2019 The Insider
3   Gilman, Ch. P. The Man-Made World, or Our Androcentric Culture. Link see next page:

in our androcentric culture looks like a straightjacket for many men with its insistence on stereotyped expectations to men to be the breadwinner, the "over-decisive", forceful, non-emotional, aggressive and fearless. In addition, men showing 'traditional female attitudes' tend to be negatively perceived since "the female" has a lower status in society. As they see it, a nation is primarily a fighting organization; and its principal business is offensive and defensive warfare. Fighting, when all is said, is for them the real business of life; not to be able to fight is to be quite out of the running.

In a certain sense, the culture of non-peace is a problem that exists within the framework of modern ideas about masculinity. Without the interest of men and without their participation, it will be very difficult to put an end to violence as the basis of a non-peace culture and create a culture of peace. Perhaps the process of emancipation of male consciousness is a more complex and delicate process than the liberation of women, but no less necessary.

One of the most encouraging trends may be an increase in the number of men who reject the patriarchy system as a system based on a culture of violence and worship of power, and who are not afraid to revise the very concept of hegemonic) masculinity and gender roles of men in a changing world. Here we see a similarity with the women's movement/feminism, which made an invaluable contribution to the reassessment of the values and gender roles of women to form a culture of peace. But the big difference between the male and female emancipation movement is that women started the struggle, being in a humiliated position and had strong motivation. Men do not have strong motivation, because most will have to abandon the obvious advantages of their status as "powerful people of this world", to awaken the suppressed (feminine?) sides of the personality and not be afraid of this "awakening of feelings", to learn to be open in communication.

What role does the policy of equal rights and equal opportunities for women and men (gender equality policy) play in this dual process – challenging man-gender norms and the formation of a culture of peace? In my opinion, the development of a culture of peace can be fueled by such a policy, as demonstrated by countries that highlight the task of creating a culture of gender equality in society and feminist foreign policy, challenging our androcentric culture.

https://seminariolecturasfeministas.files.wordpress.com/2012/01/charlotte-perkins-gilman-the-man-made-world-or-our-androcentric-culture.pdf

Here, in conclusion, I want to emphasize the persuasiveness of Virginia Woolf's "Three Guineas". Published in 1938, it remains startlingly relevant for searching a peace culture. It constituted a manifesto of reform which appeals for a change in society's patriarchal paradigm, a system claimed to be conducive to a state of affairs where violence rules. The central message of "Three Guineas" was the interconnectedness between male patriarchy, education and war. In it, Woolf gave resolutely pacifist answer to the question that occupied center stage more than seven decades ago, namely, how to protect liberty and prevent war? More specifically, how can women help in this venture? I love her answer: "We can best help you to prevent war, not by repeating your words and following your methods but by finding new words and creating new methods"[4] . What Woolf reminds us is that a culture of peace will not exist while women are kept out of power and while power is governed on the historic terms that men established in the absence of half of society.

'Searching for peace' means for me finding for new words, new (right) questions, new methods of educating and what to be taught to create a peace culture. As Woolf wrote: "Not the arts of dominating other people; not the arts of ruling, of killing, of acquiring land and capital." She continues that the college "should teach the arts of human intercourse; the art of understanding other people's lives and minds, and the little arts of talk, of dress, of cookery that are allied with them"[5] .

4   Woolf V. Three Guineas. NY: Harcourt Publishing Company. 2006. P. 131
5   Ib. P. 22-23.

SISTERHOOD AND SOLIDARITY

By Irmgard Hofer

In addition to political work, our founders started in 1919 with a lot of solidarity and charity networking. British women sent teats and suthers (all caoutchouc had been used in war) to German hospitals[1] . They bought cows in Switzerland and Netherlands and organized fodder to give it to farmers around Vienna who were obliged to give free milk to children centers and nurseries. Emily Hobhouse organized the financing of a daily school lunch in Leipzig for 11,000 children[2]. After the Zurich congress, she sent money to WILPF Germany to buy food for women in need and asked Lida Gustava Heymann to organize eggs for Gertrud Baer[3]. Aletta Jacobs (a Dutch doctor) supported health care for children in Frankfort.[4]

Clara Ragaz reminded in her welcoming words at the congress "love and respect". In her opening speech Jane Adams said: "While we approach our share in the great task with a full sense of complicity in the common disaster of the great war, may we claim, that we essay the task free from any rancorous memories of willful misunderstanding or distrust of so called enemies… May we learn from life."[5] Lida Gustava Heyman's bunch of roses to Jeanne Mélin is one symbol for the women's efforts to reconciliation. Mostly they were competing for a fair discussion.

In the Women Vote Peace project 100 years later, we continued their work in an openly declared "cooperation and solidarity across borders" and you agree hopefully when I say gratefully: Yes – we succeeded. We had no cat fight,[6] a word often used to compromise female teamwork. So I do hope, our two years old network of partners in the project will go on to bring forward the participation of women on "all levels of decision making and democracy building" in a trustful collaboration.

---

1   *Gerit v. Leitner, ,,Wollen wir unsere Hände in Unschuld waschen, Gertrud Woker" 1 Berlin 1998, p 176.*
2   *ibidem p 179.*
3   *Copies of Thanking letters to Emily Hobhouse given by Jenny Hobhouse*
4   *Damenwahl, Begleitbuch zur Ausstellung, ISBN 978-3-95542-306-3, Dankbrief OB Frankfurt E37. S. 268*
5   *Zurich 1919*
6   *Have you ever seen cats fighting? I only remember tomcats.*

WILPF Germany started a tradition 3 years ago to award "a woman rebel against war"[7] to make the public aware of physical needs and the lack of peace in parts of the world. After a Syrian and an Armenian woman, both struggling for democracy, justice and an end of the war in their country, in 2019 we awarded Rasha Jarhoum from Yemen. She stands for a solidarity movement, and started a Peace Track initiative. Yemeni women need peace, solidarity and food.

I wondered how solidarity amongst us could be strengthened. Let's start our brainstorming.

---

7   WILPF awards the "Women Rebels against War Anita-Augpurg-Prize" to women peace activists from war and crisis regions, 2017: Zaina Erham, Syria, 2018: Gulnara Shahinian, Armenia, 2019: Rasha Jarhum, Yemen; see www.wilpf.de

ZURICH CONGRESS AND WORKSHOP REKONSTRUKCJA KONGRESU EMANCYPANTEK-PACYFISTEK

By Dr Sławomira Walczewska

While men, soldiers from Germany, France, England and other countries killed each other on the fronts, women peace activists from these countries were trying already in 1915 in the Hague to find solutions how to stop the madness of war. They failed despite their courage and visionary power. Today it is time to recall the same great ideas, new thinking and visions: war is not a men's cause. Women absolutely need a voice in this matter.

In 1919, women's rights activists and pacifists from many countries met in Zurich to influence the peace process in Versailles. The power of their visions and ideas and above all their will to participate in shaping the public life, to secure political rights for women and to work for peace, are essential also today.

The five Polish founding members who participated in the congress in The Hague in 1915 were missing at the congress in Zurich in 1919. One of them, Zofia Daszyńska-Golińska, had studied economics and became the first woman to do her doctorate in economics at the University of Zurich in 1891. She knew well the way from Warsaw to Zurich, but she did not come. The reason for this was probably the Polish-Soviet War.

While peace negotiations were conducted in the West and the Western border was fixed in Poland, the war in the East continued with Soviet Russia. In 1920, Poland defended itself against the overwhelming forces of the Soviet Army and thus against its incorporation into the Soviet Union. Although the troops were already on the edge of the capital, the Red Army March towards Germany and the allied troops of Western Europe was stopped. This turnaround, marked by much effort and blood, is called "The Miracle at the Vistula" and is celebrated annually on the 15th of August. The eastern Polish border was established only in 1921 in the Riga Treaty.

The other founding member of WILPF was Maria Dulębianka, the painter and suffragette who lived in Lviv. This large, vibrant, multicultural center of the Northern Province of the Habsburg Empire became the battlefield of the growing Polish and Ukrainian nationalisms in the First World War. Dulębianka supported cooperation and reconciliation between Poles and Ukrainians. As a citizen committee, together with two other women from well-known Polish families, she has inspected the situation in the prison camps. All three women were infected with typhus and died. Dulębianka's burial turned into the Polish-Ukrainian peace demonstration.

One hundred years later in the same hotel in Zurich, we meet, feminists and pacifists from different countries. What has changed during this time? What remains? Did we make progress? We use the internet and smartphone, have mostly come by plane and everyone now has voting rights. Still, the wars are not over yet. Also in Europe, in its east, the war happens. Although women have citizens' rights, we still have far too little to say in the political decision-making bodies. A lot has changed during the hundred years, but much is still ahead of us.

"Jump over the Wall" Workshop

The concept of the "Jump Over the Wall" biographic-historical workshop was developed in eFKa[1] after many years of work with the Oral History / Herstory and later with the biographical method in adult education.

The first JOW workshops took place in 2008. The participants discussed the recent history of Europe with the split in East and West and tried to overcome this split. Later the topic was the 100th anniversary of the legalization of women's political participation, celebrated in 2018 in several Central European countries – Poland, Germany, Austria and Lithuania – and 2019 – Belgium, Hungary, Luxembourg, Georgia.

The JOW workshops focus on the interrelationships between biographical memories and cultural knowledge about the past. Critical reflection on these relationships brings with it both the growing of historical knowledge and the identification of open questions. The workshop allows the participants to experience that this kind of reflection and exchange has empowering and transforming effect.

---

1   http://efka.org.pl/sto-lat-praw-wyborczych-kobiet-warsztat-historyczno-biograficzny/

The aim of the course is to present, how to apply biographical method into empowering education. The participants try out the educational instrument. They will reflect and explore the interconnections between history/herstory and biography.

The workshop is addressed to educators, NGO-activists, gender studies academic teachers and in generally to women from East and West, South and North.

The main methods are: experience-oriented sessions, memory work, role-playing sessions, various cooperative activities based on biography/ies, discussions and short lectures between the activities, planning of transfer of the gained knowledge into own educational activity.

In Zurich this method completed the historical re-enactment and the thematic work.

CENTENARY THE 2ND CONGRESS OF WOMEN'S INTERNATIONAL LEAGUE FOR PEACE AND FREEDOM IN ZURICH

MAY Disarmament – European initiatives

By Giovanna Pagani, Italy

The congress in 1919 in Zurich requested total universal disarmament (land, sea, air) as a preventive measure and to avoid future wars. But what happened?

We emphasize to remember this courageous request now 100 years later. The experiences of the century show us that war is still a practice and militarism a "cultural" tool making operated by the industrial, military and media complex and human beings continue to follow the patriarchal logic of violence and power.

WILPFs comprehensive resolution on Militarism and our letter of 14 April 2019 for the candidates to the European Parliament elections underline that **"militarism is deforming our societies, violating rights, irreversibly damaging our environment, and devastating public health; and that the economy of war and economic warfare puts profit over people and the planet"**.

The **militarisation of the European Union** is in direct opposition to our project of **"feminist peace"**: a sustainable peace grounded in equality, justice and demilitarized security, with women peacemakers (UNSCR 1325) and the declaration of the OSCE Women's Group.

The Permanent Structured Cooperation (**PESCO**) and the European Defense Fund (**EDF**) are unacceptable.

But first of all, I want to point out the **subjection of Europe to NATO**

If WILPF intends to get involved in effective innovative policies to change the Europe of today which is at present a fortress at the service of a cynical logic of finance and war – it cannot neglect the question of the **negative impact of Euro-Atlantism** and the **devastating role of NATO** within the world geopolitics of war. It is no secret that the US never wanted a united Europe as ally at the same level. This is the objective declared by Lord Ismay, first NATO Secretary General: "Keep the Russians out, Americans in, and

Germans down". The constitution of such an alliance has given rise to another alliance, the "Pact of Warsaw (1955).

Nato is "the elefant in the room". We women must raise our voices and break the NATO Taboo.

WILPF has always been against military alliances and in 1948 started a courageous campaign to stop the creation of NATO, a military-nuclear alliance in full contradiction with one of the **primary principles of the Unite Nations: disarmament.**

After the collapse of the Berlin wall (1989) and the dissolution of the Warsaw Pact, far from being dismantled, NATO was strengthened (modification of art. 5) and transformed from being a "defensive" alliance to being an "offensive" one which, through a progressive renovation of its doctrinal and organizational scheme, became a **"war machine"** that assumes the right to impose respect of the UN Charter.

NATO, recognized as the **basis of EU defense strategy**, impedes Europe – Nobel prize for Peace in 2012! – from having independent international politics, which, in the interests of all, ought to be for the promotion of peace. Of the 27 UE countries (after Brexit), 22 belong to NATO and 4 of these are doubly bonded to NATO through the "nuclear sharing" which implies the presence of US nuclear bombs in Italy, Belgium, Holland and Germany (and outside of Europe, in Turkey).

Let us remember that it was imposed to **allied countries NOT to sign the TPNW** treaty for the prohibition of nuclear weapons (ONU 7 July 2017) and recently the one relating to commercial agreements with China for the "new silk road". **So the will of the European Parliament that voted in December 2016 in favor of a Treaty to ban the bomb was cancelled**.

NATO conditions European politics through **high military budgets** that make necessary austerity politics in other sectors and an ambiguous, transversal **civil/military promiscuity**: great military works (for example in Italy the enlargement of the military bases of Camp Darby and Ghedi) and even agreements between the army and the ministry for education to promote military culture in the schools.

NATO is controlled by the Pentagon and the US, the most militarized country in the world, which committed with impunity a crime against humanity, twice using nuclear weapons against Japan when this country had already surrendered.

NATO's expansion is a threat, not only in Europe but in the whole world (see the recent entry of Colombia as a member and the first global partner in Latin America, with other partners: Afghanistan, Iraq, Pakistan, New Zea-and, Japan, Mongolia, South Korea). **Nuclear arms** are in the center of interest (about 15.000 nuclear warheads of which about 1.800 are kept in state of alert and can be activated within 15 minutes) in synergy with **armed drones** (new systems of long distance arms), in the alarming framework of the race towards **cyber warfare** (cyber attacks and cyber robberies could lead to false alarms of an attack, or potentially even allow an enemy to take control of the nuclear arms) and towards **autonomous "intelligent" arms**.

The first World Conference for the closing of US and NATO military bases, held 16th, 18th November 2018 and co-organized by WILPF, supported this worrying data: **95% of foreign bases round the world are US and NATO** (about 1.000 military bases), present in 145 countries of which 42 are strategic, like Italy, which has 10%.

During the Conference, **Mairead Corrigan Maguire**, Nobel Peace Prize calling for a strong non violent cohesion for the closure of military bases, declared that **"NATO is a real shame on the whole international community and should be brought before the criminal court of Justice for war crimes"**.

This is our **PLAN OF ACTION for a feminist challenge for a peaceful Europe in a peaceful world:**

- Give a voice in Europe to **"victims of NATO"** (war in ex-Yugoslavia, impact of the militarization of territories, nuclear harbors) in order to witness with strength that NATO doesn't protect us, but is a threat to our life. The voices of 'hibakusha' and of the victims of nuclear tests were extremely important to the achievement of TPNW.
- Continue **stigmatizing nuclear weapons**, in order to influence the collective imagination and stimulate a deep "desire" for their total elimination.
- Motivate **representatives of municipal or regional councils and members of parliaments** to engage with ICAN in order to promote the ratification of the Treaty "ICAN Pledge" "The city for TPNW".
- Raise awareness about the **harmful effects of radiological contamination** in women and children (that are from 10 to 20 times more radiosensitive than adults and, therefore, much more exposed to cancer).
- Campaign for the **closing of USA and NATO military bases**. They are dangerous for the safety of the territory and the health of the population, they contaminate the environment and are a source of economic and political corruption.

- **Commit to contrast the European Army, to further demilitarize the EU and develop strategies for solidarity and cooperation policies.**
- Campaign in favor of **conscientious objection to military service** and to promote **Civilian Peace Corps under the UN**, with the job of training observers, mediators and specialists in the resolution of conflicts.
- Highlight the **nexus between nuclear threat and climatic threat** in order to develop a wide eco-pacifist coalition that requires the denuclearization of the planet, as a precondition for sustainable human development, based on an awareness of our alliance with nature. This theme is also at the COP 25 in Chile (December of 2019).
- Stimulate awareness on the theme of military expenses, that steal precious resources from an **economy of peace** that includes the Campaign "Don't Bank on the Bomb". **Move the money from war to peace** to get better education, culture, the satisfaction of needs and dignity in life.
- Increase the **culture of peace** to develop a planetary consciousness also through a specific activity of education (formal and informal) essential to promote: disarmament, respect for the environment, intercultural dialogue and female empowerment.
- raise a lively campaign for **educational information** in opposition to the distorted perception of the nuclear problem (based also on media distortion of reality), spreading a scientific and humanitarian approach able to connect it to the climatic threat and social injustice, involving journalists, teachers, educators, artists and social operators.
- **Promote also in Europe the 2nd World March for Peace and Nonviolence** (Madrid 2 October 2019 - Madrid 8 March 2020) which was decided with the themes: disarmament and the ratification of the TPNW, the refounding of the United Nation, the battle against every form of discrimination and violence, climatic justice and social justice. We are committed to the Campaign for a Conference for a Mediterranean Sea Free of Nuclear arms.
- Support the constitution of the Association of Ambassadors of Peace with a specific commitment addressed to the culture of dialogue through educational projects of intercultural peace, women's rights, children's rights and equal rights.
- **Reclaim the Unite Nations as a Peace organization!**

WOMEN, PEACE, DISARMAMENT AND SECURITY

By Liat Biron

The 2019 WILPF Conference in Zurich marked the 100th anniversary of the 2nd International Women's Conference. The women who convened in Zurich 100 years ago had a vision of a world without wars; the goal was not to "make war safer for women"[1], but to end wars altogether. WILPF has since worked endlessly to promote this agenda through its activities world-wide, including in the field of disarmament. The conference this year brought ideas of promoting a 'peace culture' rather than a 'military culture' in its disarmament workshop, among others. As an Israeli, born in a country considered to be one of the most militarized countries in the world[2], and among the world's top ten arms exporters, this is no easy task. Still, feminist activists persist.

---

1   *Shepherd, L. J. (2016). 'Making war safe for women? National actions plans and the militarization of the Women, Peace and Security agenda', International Political Science Review, 37(3), pp. 324-335*

2   *Mutschler, M. M. & Bales, M. (2018) Global Militarization Index. Bonn: Bonn International Center for Conversion.*

The gendered impacts of arms exceed beyond "wartime", and move from the "battlefront" to the "home-front"[3]. Women, in that aspect, are suffering the consequences of normalized armed public and private spheres, with prevalence of guns bringing more danger than security for women. However, militarized masculine understandings of 'security' tend to ignore and silence women's voices in these aspects, in a globally armed world.

The Arms Trade Treaty (ATT), adapted in 2014, was a watershed moment in the history of global gun regulation and arms control. Feminist activists made the connection between arms and gender-based violence, and the ATT included a gender provision. According to the ATT, states have to conduct a risk assessment when authorising arms exports, and one of the criteria is not to authorise the export if there is a risk that the exported weapons will be used to perpetrate 'serious acts of gender-based violence'. At the same time, CEDAW General Recommendation 30 also mentioned the direct and indirect effects that proliferation of arms has on women and girls and urged states to meet their obligations under the convention through regulating arms control, and also to sign, ratify and implement the ATT.

The Women, Peace and Security (WPS) agenda eventually made the same connection, although it took some time for disarmament to be emphasized in its resolutions. The "prevention" pillar, as several feminist scholars and activists claim, is the weakest pillar in the WPS agenda[4], compared to the pillars of "protection" and "participation". However, this is beginning to change, as demands for arms control and disarmament are slowly entering this Security Council's led initiative, as witnessed in the WPS resolutions that followed the adaption of the ATT, for example UN resolutions 2106, 2122, 2242 and the recent UNSCR 2467.

In Israel, women's organizations have created a coalition to produce and promote a WPS National Action Plan. One of the demands in the NGO-led WPS NAP is to reduce the prevalence of guns and other weapons in civil society and strengthen guns regulations. This is mostly due to the work of a coalition of feminist Israeli NGOs named "The Gun on the Kitchen Table"

3   *This is in line with the "Continuum of Violence" theory, as highlighted and conceptualized in: Cockburn, C. (2004). 'The continuum of violence: a gender perspective on war and peace' in Giles, W. and Hyndman, J. (eds) Sites of Violence: Gender and Conflict Zones. Los Angeles: University of California Press, pp. 24-44*

4   *Basu, S., & Confortini, C. (2017). Weakest "P" in the 1325 Pod? Realizing conflict prevention through security council resolution 1325. International Studies Perspectives, 18, 43–63.*

who consistently makes the connections between militarism and violence against women, a connection that is still taboo in Israel, yet is gaining more awareness worldwide. While the WPS NAP has not been implemented yet in Israel, there are countries that have successfully used their WPS NAPs for disarmament and arms control purposes, for example the Philippines that adopted their WPS NAP in 2010, following comprehensive consultations and strong advocacy by women's civil society to reduce small arms proliferation and violence, including putting small arms regulations in place in national legislation and improving the system for registration of small arms. In a militaristic society such as Israel, gun control in itself is a complex issue to raise and tackle. Although Israel has signed the ATT, it has not ratified it yet, similarly to the United States and some other remaining countries. Ratifying the ATT has been "strongly recommended" by WPS resolutions, yet this statement is still lacking stimulus. Perhaps it is time for a WPS resolution that focuses on disarmament alone – acknowledging the gendered impact that the prevalence of arms has on women, and on global peace and security. The fact that the Security Council, the author of the WPS resolutions is composed of the biggest arms exporters in the world, does not make this easier. However, WILPF's vision of a "feminist Security Council" sets high goals, also in terms of disarmament. Striving toward these goals will take time, and requires persistence and coordination both at the international and national level.

Demilitarizing the most militarized countries, disarming the biggest arms exporters. Who said that feminist activists' lives are easy? Yet feminist activists persist. At the same time, it's important to remember that the ATT, CEDAW and the WPS resolutions are all important tools that women did not have 100 years ago. Years of feminist struggles have seen results through their adaption and conceptualization. Let us utilize them as we continue striving to create a demilitarized, disarmed future.

IN THE NEXT DECADE, PEACE EDUCATION WILL HAVE TO BE GENDER AND CLIMATE SENSITIVE

Reflections based on the Workshop peace education and environmental education, Women vote peace, Zurich 2019

By Virginie Poyetton

Climate change is a defining threat to peace in the 21st century, as recently and repeatedly highlighted by the UN Security Council, the European Union and the African Union.

Today, conflicts over the use of land and resources are among the main factors in violent conflicts. The Pathways for Peace Report of the World Bank and the United Nations (UN) emphasizes that 40-60% of all domestic armed conflicts in the last 60 years have either been triggered, financed or sustained by conflicts over natural resources.

On the other hand, the Paris Agreement (COP 21) adopted in 2015 recognizes in its preamble that "when taking measures to address these changes {climate change}, Parties should respect, promote and take into account their respective obligations regarding (...) gender equality the empowerment of women (...)". As UN Women notes, however, this new legal instrument omits the role of women as agents of change. The key sections on finance, development and technology transfer do not mention gender, nor do the monitoring indicators. A year later, the 22nd International Climate Conference (COP 22) in Marrakech opened a "dialogue on the transformative implementation of gender-responsive climate solutions".

The awareness is then real: effective responses to conflict prevention and peacebuilding in countries and regions affected by climate change will therefore require **leveraging the agency of women and strengthening social inclusion** – especially of local women – who are on the frontlines of climate change, considering intersectional vulnerabilities and opportunities.

Furthermore, the UN Agenda 2030 for sustainable development, adopted in 2015, set out two goals which refer to peace, women and climate:
- The SDG 13 which aims to promote mechanisms for raising capacity for effective climate change-related planning and management in least

developed countries and small island developing States, including focusing on women, youth and local and marginalized communities.

- As well as the SDG 16 which stands for justice for all, including institutions and good governance, and aims to strengthen and promote societies capable of peace. In accordance with the Agenda 2030, the focus should therefore be on cooperation and the strengthening of cooperation and peace potentials rather than confrontation.

Concretely how should gender-responsive approaches to preventing and resolving climate conflict look like? What influence does it have on peace education?

Women as survivors and policy makers

In April 2015, the 31st Triennial Congress of the Women's International League for Peace and Freedom, meeting in The Hague recognized that climate change has a disproportionate effect on the poor, women, Indigenous peoples, coastal and small island communities, such as those in the Pacific, including Takuu, Kiribati and Tuvalu.

In fact, research shows that the poorest populations feel the impact of climate change much more strongly. Women, who have a higher chance to belong to these populations, are therefore logically on the front line:

- In the event of natural disasters, the risk of death is 14 times higher for women and children.
- In countries with the highest gender inequalities, four times as many women as men die in floods.
- More than 70% of those killed by the Asian tsunami were women.
- Hurricane Katrina in the United States in 2005 affected mostly African-American women, the poorest community in the New Orleans region .

Gender norms therefore play a key role in women's vulnerability to climate change. Since the burden of collecting water, food and fuel rests mainly on women and girls, the time they spend on these tasks is multiplied in the case of drought or floods. This can have negative consequences on their schooling and working lives.

In the event of natural disasters, women have a limited ability to react due to social norms that prevent them, for example, from leaving their homes without a male guardian. In addition, they are rarely taught the survival skills commonly taught to boys, such as swimming or climbing.

This being said, women are not only survivors of climate change. Given their role in natural resource management and the responsibilities they often have in providing energy to their households, they are key players in mitigation and adaptation to climate change.

Nevertheless, their contributions are rarely recognized, even though research shows that societies fare better after a natural disaster when women participate in the development of early warning systems and reconstruction efforts.

The latest news have also showed that women often stand against the destruction of nature and the environment in the front line. The Youth for climate movement is a good example of how young women – such as: Greta Thunberg (Sweden), Luisa Neubauer (Germany), Claire Renauld (France)- can guide public debate and defend environmental and human rights. These young women found the courage to speak for themselves, for their future, for the future of the next generations.

Implications for environmental and peace education

How should peace education adjust to these new challenges? How could the diversity of roles played by women in responding climate change? How can peace education recognize and support women's leadership and enhance their knowledge in climate change adaptation and mitigation? How can it encourage the participation of women in climate change policy making at local, national and international levels?

The answer is complex and requires a multilevel approach. However, Peace education should be able at least to address the following three dimensions of climate solutions with a women's rights, agency and gender equality perspective:

- Technical: renewables, water-saving adaptation technologies.etc.
- Non-technical: consumption changes, social changes, values, denial and disinformation etc.
- Transformational: addressing governance, institutional and political change, planning processes

In summary, the challenge of peace education in the next decades will be to promote a conflict transformative and gender sensitive approach to climate change.

FROM SUPPORTING CONSCIENTIOUS OBJECTORS
TO BECOMING CONSCIENTIOUS PROTECTORS OF THE EARTH

Women as Change Agents then and now 1919-2019

By Roslyn Cook

The women gathered together in Zurich at the 2019 Congress shared a lively appreciation of the significant moments they were re-enacting from 100 years earlier. Familiar with the poignant tales of having travelled long distances across a war torn landscape, they were united by bonds of sisterhood and their determination to uphold a vision of what the world could be like if only they be heard; we knew their stories and on that day we were them.

Daring to seek participation in political life on an equal footing with men those women were felt to have been truly heroic and deserving of a recognition resonant with our own challenging times. The mission now no less urgent, passion and hope riding on the belief that a gendered sensibility based on the need for compassion and humanity could, would and will make the crucial difference in addressing the misery of war, the degradation of the environment and the restoration of the most basic resources required to sustain life.

No surprise then that the workshop that took place on the Saturday afternoon concerning Peace Education and Climate justice focussed minds on how the Women's International League for Peace and Freedom might achieve maximum impact in bringing about positive change 100 years later, with the urgent need to confront the two major threats to life on earth, climate change and nuclear weapons.

Cue the International Law against Ecocide – a law that would make it a crime to destroy the environment and would hold individuals to account for doing so whether they be government ministers or CEOs of corporations, whether their actions or policies caused such damage or were deemed to risk doing so. Perpetrators of Ecocide could be prosecuted at the International Criminal Court where it would be the Fifth Crime Against Peace.

Hardly anyone at the workshop had heard of it, although it had been discussed at the UN for decades it was successfully forgotten until one day a barrister, the late Polly Higgins, looked out of a court room window and decided the Earth needed a good lawyer. She named this new crime Ecocide, unaware it had already been thought of and had been promoted by the Swedish prime minister, Olaf Palme. She discovered it had in fact been included on the original draft of the Rome Statute but was dropped abruptly in 1996, the same year the illegality of nuclear weapons had come under scrutiny. An idea whose time had surely come found new life as Polly dedicated hers to making it a reality.

She had presented her definition of Ecocide to the UN in 2010:

Ecocide crime is: acts or omissions committed in times of peace or conflict by any senior person within the course of State, corporate or any other entity's activity which cause, contribute to, or may be expected to cause or contribute to serious ecological, climate or cultural loss or damage to or destruction of ecosystem(s) of a given territory(ies), such that peaceful enjoyment by the inhabitants has been or will be severely diminished. https://eradicatingecocide.com/the-law/the-model-law/

It was apt that I first met Polly at the People Power conference in 2011, where she had eloquently advocated her vision of a world made safer by a simple idea and a belief in the potential that we all inherently possess to realise and give voice to our own power. As a campaigner for the abolition of nuclear weapons which threaten the ultimate Ecocide, I found we were instantly on the same page. What was needed was new law, and for consciousness to shift just as it had when slavery was abolished.

Thanks to Polly's work the International Law against Ecocide now has a growing movement of supporters known as Earth Protectors. Those arrested as part of the recent civil disobedience during Extinction Rebellion as well as those opposing fracking have had the chance to supplement their defence in court with the Earth Protectors Trust Fund document as proof that they acted as Conscientious Protectors of the Earth – a term coined by Polly.

It was indeed poetic to be representing a Quaker from 1919 at the Congress who had been dedicated to supporting Conscientious Objectors in their refusal to fight in the war, deeply concerned to address the suffering of those affected by it and to ensure that the terms of the Peace treaty would not lead to another one.

Like a poem in the process of being written I felt particularly driven to share Polly's vision of a million Earth Protectors signing up, making Ecocide law a reality at the 11th hour for the Earth, after her untimely death at the age of 50 just two weeks earlier that had shocked those who knew her to the core. Whilst processing the grief we felt collectively the urgency expressed during the protests in London that April meant her legacy had suddenly achieved the profile she had worked so hard for ten years to create. A large banner at her funeral read "Polly is everywhere", I felt she was with me in Zurich for sure.

With what I have come to name the power of Polly, talk of how an International Law against Ecocide would change the game and how we in WILPF could recruit Earth Protectors ignited energetic discussion and our workshop unanimously agreed WILPF should promote it going forwards. It was also acknowledged that this law would automatically reinforce the 2017 UN Treaty to Prohibit Nuclear Weapons, which WILPF already strongly supports as a partner of the International Campaign to Abolish Nuclear Weapons (ICAN). See www.nuclearban.org and www.icanw.org

To become an Earth Protector a small fee will make you a legal Trustee of the Earth, paying into a Trust Fund. The money is ring fenced to support the Small Island states in the Pacific, both financially and with effective legal expertise, so that they can get to the International Criminal Court in The Hague to table an amendment to the Rome Statute proposing an International Law Against Ecocide, something any member state could do. These states are threatened by rising sea levels due to the effects of climate change brought on by dangerous industrial activity, but this is not being recognised by the international community. Vanuatu is one such state and has taken the lead in following Polly's initiative. The support of just two thirds of member states would be required to pass an amendment into law and no state could veto it. To have law against Ecocide proposed, made public and visible would in itself spark a major shift globally in the mindset of what is possible and urgently necessary. See www.stopEcocide.earth for details.

The Earth Protectors Trust Fund document states:

"Becoming a trustee of this document is to become an Earth Protector and Trustee of Earth. It is a declaration of love and acknowledgement that the Earth, the ecosystems of Earth and inhabitants of Earth, whether human or otherwise, have the right to peaceful enjoyment. It is a declaration of belief that this peaceful enjoyment is both a moral and legal right, and that any human act or omission which severely diminishes such peaceful enjoyment is a crime.

Becoming a Trustee of Earth is to become a protector of a law which is in alignment with a universally recognised moral code of respect, peace and duty of care for all life. It is a direct expression of intent to create peace between all beings."

Our workshop concluded that peace education needs to connect the importance of climate and environmental justice with opposing militarism. This is exactly what the coalition of forces at the DSEI arms fair demonstrated in September 2019 in London. Activists from Extinction Rebellion are joining forces with those opposing the arms trade and the continued deployment and manufacture of nuclear weapons. Often of course these are the same people and all the more often they are women.

I am delighted that the work of Polly Higgins will feature at the Autumn Seminar of WILPF in London this November, demonstrating how the determination and innovative approach of one visionary woman has captured the imagination of environmentalists and peace activists alike, with a solution that inspires unity and a shared vision of how the earth could be protected for future generations. Anti-war, human rights and environmental activists can find common cause in supporting the International Law against Ecocide. Let us work together to make it the Fifth Crime against Peace.

Outcomes going forwards from Zurich Congress 2019

Workshop held on Saturday 11th May on Peace Education and Climate Justice

- Peace education connecting the importance of climate and environmental justice and opposing militarism
- Change the narrative using storytelling, humour, NVC, the arts, empathy, solidarity
- Support the Law of Ecocide as 5th Crime against Peace by recruiting Conscientious Protectors of the Earth and support the Treaty to Prohibit Nuclear Weapons
- Share best practices with a positive vision for the future

GENDER JUSTICE IN BUSINESS – SOME FEMINIST REFLECTIONS

Annemarie Sancar, WIDE Switzerland, CSP Working group Gender

Which forces can develop economic processes and how social structures can be changed and/or destroyed: is it via a feminist-motivation or via social criticism. 100 years ago women struggling for peace demanded an immediate cessation of arms traffic and war materials. It was clear that war is part of a disastrous economic and political development, which destroys societies. This is true even today, but the profit-maximizing and profit-making economy has gained the upper hand systematically in times of globalization and digitalization. Where are the networks of solidarity, where are the women, who do the most care and housework, more and more often unpaid, invisible, unspectacular? What does "peace" mean when the distribution of work and time is so unfair, the options for participation of women and men so unequal? 100 years later, women commit themselves and work together for a gender-equitable and sustainable peace!

On June 14th 2019, Switzerland saw the biggest strike for years: it was the second women's strike. The traditional forces were present, although less on the street than in new news – among them manager (women) of companies, economically successful employers and conservative politicians calling for "equal wage for equal work" and more women in economic and political leadership positions. However, there were the strong voices of feminists, which underlined some other inacceptable inequalities: The volume of unpaid work, the lion's share of which is provided by women and its value for the national economy of Switzerland, officially calculated and published! Due to the broad acceptance, that care economy is adding value to the GDP, the implications of the gendered division of labour and the related inequalities became an issue of interest. Of course, the question of how to address the issue was controversially discussed – along political lines and economic positions. Still, the majority would agree that unequal wage is inacceptable and that the discrimination of women in pension schemes as to be stopped.

In Switzerland, as in many other European countries, gender equality is enshrined constitutionally. However, in real live, it is different. Gender is still used as a category of non-justified discrimination, reflected in statistics, which shows that per year women earn 100 billion Swiss franc less than men do. The monetary value of unpaid work is 408 billion per year. Women provide more than 60% of the unpaid care work. Like Switzerland, many of the rich countries suffer from the same discrepancies and would show similar numbers. The numbers are not random though, but a product of economic dynamics and political power relations. A sound understanding of the interfaces of different stakeholders. These are the private sector (market), the government (public sector), the civil society and the households. Now, for us it is key to analyse these interrelations in order to plan actions for a change towards gender justice. Do we know what happens to profit, values and wealth generated and accumulated through our economic performance? How balanced is the share when comparing time we invest in work and what we are paid for it? Do we understand how government handles its budget? Do we understand the logical frame of financial politics, the resulting public spending and its impact on the wellbeing of the people? Last but not least, we have to understand the gendered dimension of economic and financial processes reflecting the interaction of the state, private sector, civil society and of persons in their different roles as members of households, citizens, women's activists, children, farmers, entrepreneurs, consumers etc.

These are the key questions; too many to tackle in this short input, but having these questions in mind in our continuous work may give us some guidance.

Let me quickly come back to the women's strike in Switzerland, an important symbolic moment to reinforce women's rights. At the strike, the quality of daily living conditions at micro level was an issue as much as the underlying structures of discrimination. Activists criticized the endless desire for profit maximization of the private sector, but also reflected the role of the state and the tension between industry and state. As said before, the positions differed a lot, indicating the controversy between neoliberal and critical "feminists": On one side is the narrative of self-responsibility such as "If you really want to become a successful business woman you can do it". On the other side, the critical feminist approach addresses the economic situation of women and men from a quite different angle, focusing on the underlying power relations and its gendered dynamics. Looking at individual stories and economic carriers of women or men, we only see the surface and not the conditions under which individuals perform. These are mainly the underlying mechanisms of gender specific discrimination and exploitation of labour force constituted and reproduced in the patriarchal hierarchies. Focusing on the gender specific dimension of digitalization, unemployment and the wage trends in the formal labour market. They pointed out the limited accessibility of social security system and care infrastructure to women and their relevance for women's wellbeing. Feminist activists' quintessence of these insights and discussions is probably that business both causes and replicates the underlying patriarchal structure because it corresponds with the logic of the profit-oriented market and finally benefit from economic advantages – regardles of the number of women as business leaders.

First, I will glance behind the scenes of the market. Then I will look at the performance of the state in its role as duty bearer in relation to the human and women's rights. Finally, I question the visibility and value of care work as the key activity for people's wellbeing.

Business and the question of benefits

The organization of the private sector is based on its productivity and the maximization of profit. There are different ways to increase productivity: Rationalization of production, investment in new technology, or simply by influencing the costs of the labour force such as staff redundancy, flexibilisation of contracts, informalisation of certain jobs etc. The costs for the staff should remain low, is even decreasing while the annual profit is increasing. Otherwise, the business would collapse; unfortunately, all companies are organized according to this logic. Of course, many companies have a strong human rights based performance; they do guarantee decent jobs, social security, ILO-confirm standards. Still, when it comes to the annual reporting and a company is faced with a decline in growth, it will have to respond, and the easiest way to respond is to reduce staff costs. If the legal protection of employees is weak and the logic of the tax system is rather strengthening the private sector with its financial privileges than the individual employee investing labour force. However, not all type of work is equally exposed to such changes. It also depends, as we all know, on the options that digitalization offers a company. It depends on the sectors of work and on the education and learning opportunities of the employees. We know the market is volatile, and the small enterprises with little resources for risk management are especially affected by this volatility. Their flexibility and adaptability is on average much lower compared to big national and multinational companies. Why do I underline this difference? When we talk about women's economic empowerment, in general we do not mean the high-level business leadership, but rather small entrepreneurship as a possibility for women to improve their standard of living. Women receive capacity building and small credits and as prudent savers, women repay their micro credits after investing them profitably. Women are therefore also a welcome target group for micro-credit programmes and finance institutes.

However, if we look closer at this picture, we will see that their options for investment remain very limited. First, their profits are low, often the costs are higher than the income, and only few women have control of the means of production. Without the possibilities to accumulate capital, their empowerment is in danger and instead of growing; their enterprise may shrink and disappear. Furthermore, the sectors where women perform their market-oriented activities, or where the promoting programmes of the Women Economic Empowerment-Strategy are anchored, are often subjected to crisis and economic downturns. The marge de manoeuvre is shrinking, the risk of self-exploitation increasing, which of course threatens the wellbeing of businesswomen and their families.

For those reasons, the integration of women into the market does not automatically lead to empowerment and enhanced opportunities to act in all fields of public and private fields as a rights holder. New forms of dependencies and discrimination emerge, often not visible at the first glance. Social networks break apart. The lack of time and increasing duties to fulfil push women into precarious situations. For small entrepreneurs, high pressure of the market, competitiveness and the pressure to accelerate the production for more profit, increasing quality requirements and hygiene standards, conformed by state laws, may lead to unprofitable business and high depth burden.

The dynamics at the interface of time use, labour and household budgets are very complex and dynamic, but they are decisive for gender relations. They influence and form the gender specific conditions of daily life including care work. Unfortunately, in research and politics, this remains a black box, kept under the carpet or make the gender differences invisible.

Considering the enormous power, the owners of business and market forces can display, it is for us, as feminists, an imperative to observe critically the impacts on human rights and gender justices. We have to analyse the origins and games of power and the decision-making procedures to detect popping up of new discrimination and its reproduction. We have to understand the frames of reference for politics. Are women more likely to be on the loser side than men are, when neoliberal economies dominate political decisions? How gender biased is the impact of the accelerated market system on social politics? These questions lead me to the next point.

Women's rights, human rights and the duty of the state

The direct impact of structural changes on companies, the loss of economic force of certain small enterprises in some specific branches such as the clothing industry, of which the big majority of owners are female, may hit men and women similarly, of course in relation to the differences between sectors where mainly women or men respectively work. It depends on the revalidation of their labour force, of their productivity, and on the fact that in many sectors, women's jobs are time consuming, slow and often even not suitable for rationalization. Yet, there is a second dimension, and here we switch now to my second point, the question of human and women's rights. I would dare to say, that as an indirect influence of such structural changes the living conditions of women will worsen more than men's, women will have less benefits looking at the work load they are carrying in addition to the paid job.

Businesswomen working in small enterprises will hardly ever be protected with good social security schemes. Balancing the benefits women have from being economically active on the market and the standard of living as a whole and at long term, including the reproductive or care costs, the results are rather disappointing. Women entrepreneurs invest a lot of time and money. They need support at home to care for their children, elderly relatives, or sick members in the family. They have to plan for the time after, etc. If the state is not able to support them adequately, if there is no general pension or social security system, no social infrastructure such as nursery, public hospitals or retirement homes, the huge share of this care work will fall back on women again. The essentialised role society gives women as carers by nature will compel them to organize, deliver and guaranty the provision for the fundamental services – to prevent society from a collapse?

The value added for regional and local development may decrease, may be stumbled by conflict and war, but care work is still the key for the survival, it is the basic economic activity because it produces labour force and it is the motor of social development. Therefore, the question is not about the relevance of care work, but of how it is organized and who is responsible to insure the basic care service according to human rights and women's rights and how the states can play their key role as duty barer and warrantor of a caring society.

Currently we observe the weakening of many states, and shrinking space for persons acting as members of the civil society. We also miss a systematic reporting on the human rights. At the same time, we are all somehow challenged by the withdrawal of public services, cut offs in the social sector, shrinking accessibility of the public care services. Of course, it is the state, which carries the main responsibility and we are the citizens. Still, it is more complex than that, because it is the interaction of public and private sector, the civil society and the households as said before.

The state uses powerful instruments such as budgets, tax system, and important to underline here, the <u>legal frames of the public finance system, including social security as well as tax schemes</u>. National economy allows certain insights into the economic validation of care work by the government: How much of public money is invested in schools, health service, in elderly pension schemes or day care for children and sick people compared to other so-called profitable sectors. What are the narratives justifying the cutbacks in social security and services. We all know the stories about the important role of the mother, of the wife and the capabilities caring for others – even if it is invisible, unpaid and unprotected. The protagonists of such narratives are the family and social security politics, that are generating and reproducing these narratives. Still, the politics are not storytellers, but a mirror of the national economy trends. However, do we know who from civil society is supporting this politics and why, what are the interests behind it?

Care is costly, we know, and it doesn't' generate immediate profit. Only the long-term perspective may allow calculating its economic value. However, we expect from a functioning state to ensure a public care service is inclusive and accessible without discrimination! It is also a duty of a government to assure, that the aspects of the fiscal policy are adapted, among others the tax law.

What is the message for feminists? We reclaim a political system that provides the support of care providers, based on the added value in terms of time and labour. We advocate for a changing investment strategy of the government to increase the corporate- and profits taxes of companies in order to raise the capital for social care infrastructure and therefore of course we advocate for a legal system which favours this qualitative change of direction, a state have to go.

Here I would like to quote one of the most brilliant feminist researcher Sharah Razavi (2010): "The need to address care through public policy is now more urgent than ever. Women's massive entry into the paid workforce – a near-global trend – has squeezed the time hitherto allocated to the care of family and friends on an unpaid basis. At the same time, population ageing in some countries, and major health crises (especially HIV and AIDS) in others, have intensified the need for care services." Here I would add also the costs of long lasting conflicts, war and militarization! Shahra points out that in many countries public health systems have been severely weakened during the decades of market-oriented reform, and we know that the same is true in the OSCE participating States, that much of the care burden has fallen back on women and girls.

Shahra Razavi concludes by underlying the specific role of the state: it is qualitatively different from that of the private sector, civil society of the households as main actors in the provision of basic care. It is not just a provider of public care services, but also a significant decision maker when it comes to the rights and responsibilities of other institutions. Whether and how the state makes use of its role is fundamental for defining who has access to quality care and who bears the costs of its provision. The effective creation, regulation and funding of care services can increase the access, affordability and quality of care and reduce time burdens placed on unpaid care-givers. Parental leaves, family allowances and other transfers can be financed through taxes or social insurance programmes, thereby socializing some of the costs assumed by unpaid caregivers. From a feminist perspective, the focus lies on the relation between the market value of labour in relation to the time used for it on one side and the resulting productivity-gap between paid and unpaid care work on the other side. The findings show it clearly: there is a strong gender bias, where women turn out to be the losers, especially those providing hours of care work unpaid and invisible. Their productivity is not valorised as such. In addition, the government also misses to compensate for it, be it in form of a fundamental rights based public services or through subsidies for non-profit organizations and services deliverers of care services.

Conclusion

New trends in business and markets are alarming and many feminists are worried about the possible new forms of discrimination. There are many reasons to worry: The rationalization and digitalization of modes of production, the dismissals in certain sectors, the increasing expenditure for the army and high tech security technology, the destabilizing impact of austerity programs in the social sector: All these developments and trends have a strong gender dimension. Gender is an immanent category of the logic and the structures behind. This has a high prize, which becomes clear when we look at the quality of life. Who are the losers, who the winners, and how gendered is this gap! Women will not be affected the same way as men are, and their chances will not increase in the same way as men's will – especially also as economic actors. Individual stories give insights into these discrepancies. However, to understand them, we should not reach for explanations such as individual responsibility, incapacities or even laziness, but analyse the social economic causes of discrimination – in the context we work in, we deal with, we know and may be able to influence. Women's rights are the key. Women have the same rights to care as men do, independently of the benefit they add to the private sector. It is not a question of the rate of return but of a fundamental right. Care work is an economic activity adding value to the gross domestic product of a state. It is this value, which has to be reconsidered and taken as a benchmark, and not as the rate of return. There is no justification for not including it in the GDP, not even the female capability of being loving mothers.

WOMEN IN INFORMAL ECONOMY: ACTUALITIES, VULNERABILITIES – A NEED FOR COMPREHENSIVE PROTECTION.

By Gulnara Shahinian "Democracy Today"

Current political processes, registered a sharp decline in human rights protection and social guaranties, raise concerns on its implications towards protection for all and especially those women and men, whose labor is highly demanded in the modern labor market, but typically invisible, unprotected and vulnerable to such challenges – women and men in informal labor.

This well-known phenomenon calls for stronger responsibility of states to address this structural injustice through rethinking labor and human security and gender equality policies, look into the development of viable protection mechanisms, innovative methodologies to meet the rising challenges. .

Having a very long history, this type of labor is on the rapid rise in the modern world. It takes a variety of forms and definitional shades from the residual ones in the form of still existing slavery, bonded labor and other "slavery-like "situations emerging in shadows of home economies and the rise in their modern equivalents. In Eastern Europe and CIS countries, it had its special expressions after the collapse of the Soviet planned system of economy and authoritarian forms of governance. Let me name some examples from our region: Initiated by women as temporary "proactive" survival "strategies" after this collapse forms of shadow occupation such as "shuttle trade", or art craft makers, home bakers, or so much demanded migrant domestic and care workers. Sadly, to note that these existential strategies initiated by women as temporary survival measures happened to have a "long life" and even alongside with the other forms of informal work some transmuted into new forms of dangerous unprotected labor that moved women from shops to street sidewalks or turned onto serfs on agricultural lands.

The majority of this is unprotected; risky informal labor is unaddressed, unnoticed and represents the enormous loss of intellectual, educational and creative power and potential for the society. The important group of employed in the informal economy are migrant workers, the majority of whom according to researchers are women. The jobs they find are often precarious, with restrictive migration policies and labor laws in some countries even tying immigration status to labor contracts such as Kafala in The Gulf States or type of labor contract in Great Britain, which puts women in complete dependence from employers enslaving them, leaving them without any right to bargain their situation.

International protection related to domestic workers developed and adopted by the states is rarely enforced and evoked in courts in many countries.

According to ILO more than 2 billion women and men around the world are in informal labor which makes about two-thirds of the modern workforce (ILO 2018). To classify the phenomena I will use an operational definition of ILO provided in International Labor Conference Recommendation 204 (2015). This definition "considers all people working in an unregistered business (whether the owner or an employee); contributing household workers; and own accounts workers and employees without a recognized employment relationship to be in informal employment."

The statistic is immense, though realistically it is even much higher when we speak on hidden, shadow incalculable activity such as informal labor, which is not always easy to identify. Informality makes people almost invisible and harder to reach through mainstream institutional interventions in protecting their rights and social inclusion.

In current times global economies, political systems' social relations are in a process of fluctuations and turbulence and instability. Name just some: climate change, economic recession, unprecedented scale of migration, conflicts, and wars, sharp decline in human rights protection strongly observed in the recent years, raise in tribalism and residual and emerging colonial attitudes are issues of global transnational concerns that provide complex impact on lives of people and gender relations and especially the most vulnerable. The globalization of value chains and government cuts to social spending are just some of the factors that push people into informal employment. Peculiarly enough global policies are echoed by restrictive policies by the states that impact all, specifically women.

The increase of conflicts and wars and change in their nature has also a strong impact on gender roles in society enhancing inequality and making it even more pronounced than in other operating environments.

There have been several studies and reports underscoring that during conflicts opportunities for gender-based discrimination and violence increase as systems are weakened and protection almost absent. Women in conflict situations are 'disproportionately exposed to sexual violence', which can include trafficking of women and girls for sexual exploitation and child labor. Similarly, in post-conflict situations, women and girls are at greater risk of trafficking-related sexual exploitation and gender-based violence.

In its reports the UN stresses that conflict and post-conflict situations can disproportionately affect women's access to, and management of land and other natural resources because of their reliance on these resources for their livelihoods and their responsibility for fulfilling their families' needs. UN Working Group on Business and Human Rights, in its report, noted that 'some business platforms suggest that addressing root causes is the next frontier for businesses. However, there is a pronounced tendency by some industry leaders in limiting their responsibility for the social protection of workers and some national governments trying to cut social spending.

This global pattern seemed to be encouraged under the policies of international organizations. For example, in the 1990s, World Bank and IMF reforms obliged recipient countries to incorporate more "flexibility" into their labor codes. As a result, the traditional provision of social security has been returned to workers themselves, who shift into a life of declining earnings and with their rights and their ability to organize themselves undermined. The net result is that hundreds of millions of workers have themselves absorbed the non-wage costs of production and as a result live below poverty lines with little or no social protection.

The sequence of unsafety caused by these factors adds up to an increase in vulnerabilities and exploitative working conditions in informal sectors. Women are not necessarily more likely to be engaged in informal employment than men, but in the informal sector the occupations, job security, and incomes of women tend to be different from those of men (ILO, 2018). It has to be stressed that women experience vulnerability because they are women and then working in an informal economy.

While there has been developed number of international legal instruments addressing informal labor directly or through some articles, international law such as ILO convention 182 on domestic workers, ILO convention 177 on Homework, Convention on rights of migrant workers and their families and recommendations of UN CEDAW, UN Palermo Protocol to prevent, punish and suppress trafficking in humans, domestic protection is still weak, inexistent or not enforced. The UNGPs are the first global set of guidelines on business and human rights, are seen as a cornerstone of the business and human rights, and are understood in the context of State obligations of nondiscrimination and their regulation of companies and non-state actors. Despite the importance of women in the business and human rights context, there is very limited mention of the issue in the UNGPs. However, they make a brief mention of the unique risks women face, among a list of other groups, but of course no mentioning shadow economy workers.

These Guiding Principles should be implemented in a non-discriminatory manner, with particular attention to the rights and needs of, as well as the challenges faced by, individuals from groups or populations that may be at heightened risk of becoming vulnerable or marginalized, and with due regard to the different risks that may be faced by women and men.

There have been numerous cases registered in several countries when women's informal employment turned to exploitation and trafficking and or cases of migrant domestic workers reported to be killed or raped. Many such criminal acts against domestic workers have been registered with no responses from the Governments, with some traditional explanations that the women have traveled informally, or no diplomatic relations between the states to solve the issue or the law does not have extraterritorial coverage.

Protective framework for informal workers is inexistent or even if it is there is not implemented: neither their working environment nor they receive protection under health and safety regulation, no secure contracts and protection under the law. Women are vulnerable to various forms of exploitation by employers, such as forced labor and sexual exploitation and trafficking as they often work without written contracts or fake ones. In Ghana women porters who were coming with their small children to capital to work as porters had to sleep together with their children in market space under the open air. Cases of violence, rape, and robing have been quite frequent. Benefits such as overtime pay, a minimum wage, paid vacation and sick leave, health insurance, unemployment insurance, maternity benefits, and parental leave do not exist for them. They have little or no formal means of managing risk, are not covered with pension benefits or access to childcare. They experience double discrimination first as women, second as informal workers. As was mentioned previously women dominate the informal economy though according to studies even in such risky jobs women's income is lower than men's.

It is widely assumed that informal workers operate outside the realm of labor laws. In many countries, the existing laws are punitive and they are excluded from the protection by law, their livelihoods are compromised as well human rights violated. Often they become subjects of police harassment and are treated as criminals. Policies toward informal workers in some countries solely are addressed in the realm of poverty alleviation projects, particularly for women. While there have been developed many models to address the rights of informal workers, they are rarely implemented and are gender blind.

In conclusion, I will present some recommendations.

The policy of social inclusion and gender equality are the keys to address the existing in the field structural injustice which requires to maximally embrace informal sector in the provision of social protection schemes, such as health insurance, pensions, and maternity benefits, improving occupational safety and reducing work hazards, improving access to childcare. It is important to "formalize the existence of workers in the shadow economy" through building informal workers' organizations, alliances, and networks which are some of the ways that can be undertaken to improve the conditions of informal workers, especially women. Improving the conditions of informal workers, therefore, must have to take a gendered approach. **States must demonstrate** due diligence in protecting the workers in this area of labor. This is a social dialogue between state and it's citizens. **The weak market-friendly policies and declarations will not help here.** The strong local regulatory framework that protects the rights of informal workers will invest in economic development that will allow them to achieve their full potential.

Formalizing the informal economy means providing voice and recognizing economic power and realizing decent work for the informal economy, which in turn will build the capacity and organizational strength to claim rights as citizens and workers. Addressing the conditions of female informal workers contributes to poverty reduction as it means improving the lives of at least half of the working population in many countries. Improving living and working conditions of female informal workers will invest in raise in their productivity and increased the income that contributes to overall economic growth, and reduces poverty in the long term. Gender inequity in the informal economy must be taken into account in development planning. Such action will contribute to aiding effectiveness. Being good such policies need to be taken with special care not to allow collateral damage and leave the decision to women, as many are involved in informal work based on their decision. So it requires also enhancing the confidence of people in the state system.

Another interesting proposal will be introducing universal basic income, the policy that found it's very good results in some countries and which provided people with better stability and choice.

Some promising practices developed in the field: Global Compact and UN Women have introduced women's empowerment principles as a joint undertaking on how businesses can respect women's rights and support women's empowerment. CEOs from 604 companies have signed on thus far. 7 principles cut across the promotion of women's leadership and entrepreneurship, education, and training, equal opportunities and nondiscrimination in the workplace as well as laws that protect their health and safety and protect them exploitation. They also promote transparency, measuring and reporting on these key issues

Another example is use of Maastricht Principles on Extraterritorial Obligations of States in the area of Economic, Social and Cultural Rights to protect the rights of migrant workers which is a set of principles adopted by a set of international human rights experts and represent a consensus view as to where international law is at in terms of States extraterritorial obligations. While they focus on State obligations and the behavior of businesses overseas, they incorporate principles of gender equality. Specifically, the responsibility of States extends to acts and omissions of non-state actors. Additionally, the Maastricht Principles require that States observe human rights principles relevant to women such as the right to participate in decision-making, non-discrimination and gender equality.

AUTHOR'S SHORT BIOGRAFIES

Ketevan Bakradze

born in 1993 in Tbilisi / Georgia; bachelor in sociology at the Iwane-Dscha-wachischwili-University Tbilisi and in a funded exchange program in Germany and Austria. Since 2016, she lives in Vienna/Austria and does her master in Gender Studies at the Vienna university on homophobia and nationalism in Georgia. She is project partner in "Women vote Peace"

Liat Biron

is a Politics and Government Doctoral Candidate in the University of Ben Gurion and the CEO of the Forum for Regional Thinking. She is a feminist antimilitarist activist and an expert on Gender, Peace and Security, and has worked for several years in refugee and displaced persons camps in South Sudan, focusing on response to and prevention of violence against women in conflict zones. Liat holds a BA in Communication, MA in Public Policy from Tel Aviv University and MSc in Women, Peace and Security from the London School of Economics and Political Science. She is a graduate of the WIZO Women Leadership Program in cooperation with the US Embassy and of the Clinton Center for Peace. She is currently working to revive the WILPF branch in Israel.

Roslyn Cook

is a writer and campaigner with WILPF and on the Campaign for Nuclear Disarmament National Council, both partners of the International Campaign for the Abolition of Nuclear Weapons (ICAN). She is also an Ambassador for StopEcocide, an organisation working to institute the International Law against Ecocide as the Fifth Crime against Peace at the International Criminal Court. She holds a BA Honours degree in History with German from the School of European Studies at the University of Sussex, where she also studied Life History and Life Writing at Masters level.

Ite van Djik

Born in The Hague, The Netherlands, 1949; Professional work as legal aid lawyer for 20 years, as policy staff member of the Dutch Data Protection Authority and as policy adviser of the Dutch Human Rights Institute the rights of women, refugees and migrants played an important role.

As feminist since the 70s, active for equality law, abortion rights, policies to combat trafficking in women, political empowerment, and, since my retirement, for WILPF NL and WILPF EU. Working closely with other women has given me a lot of satisfaction, by sharing feminist analyses, by dealing with differences in view and by experiencing solidarity and friendship.

Irmgard Hofer

is a retired special education teacher. Her engagement in women's and peace movement led her 1995 to WILPF/IFFF. She participated in WILPF'S peacetrain from the 80-years-congress in Helsinki to the UN women's congress in Bejing. She is president of the German section since 2001 and works in different networks for disarmament.

Dr Maki Kimura

is a job share International Liaison Officer of the Women's International League for Peace and Freedom (WILPF) UK. Maki, originally from Japan and now based in the UK, has extensive experience in teaching and research in the area of gender. She is the author of the book on Japan's Military Sexual Slavery during the Second World War ('comfort women') Unfolding the 'Comfort Women' Debates: Modernity, Violence, Women's Voices (2016) Basingstoke: Palgrave Macmillan, and continues her research into war, gender and memory. She is also a founding member of Justice of 'Comfort Women' UK which aims to raise the awareness of the issue of 'comfort women' in the UK. She is project partner in "Women vote Peace"

Carmen Magallón

considers herself an academic/activist or an activist/academic rejecting the dichotomy: University Professor in the Area of Arts and Humanities, graduated in Physics; Master degree studies in History and Philosophy of Science. She worked as Director of SIP Foundations, a Peace Research center, based in Zaragoza, Spain (2003-2018). Currently is the President of that foundation: www.seipaz.org. CM was a member of Women in Black in Spain and of the Council of War Resisters' International. She has been Vice-president of AIPAZ (Spanish Research for Peace Association). In 2011, with a group of women founded the WILPF Spain section. She is project partner in "Women vote Peace"

Andrea Marikovszky

Artist, art teacher, activist, a member of The First Hungarian Society for Basic Income, and the only Hungarian member of WILPF right now. She lives in Budapest as a single mother with three children. As an activist she has worked for women's right movement since the 90's for the development of birth care, and also the education system. She arranged mentor programs for teachers, working for children with special needs. She regularly organizes feminist events for the public as her main interest is in social imaginary and the feminist future, and publishes articles in Hungary in connection with these topics.

Heidi Meinzolt

Member of the Board of WILPF, responsible for the European region.In Germany, she is a founding member of the "Women's security Council" promoting the implementation of UNSCR1325 and the Women-Peace-and-Security Agenda/WPS. Since 2016, she coordinates the Working Group on Women&Gender realities in the Civic Solidarity Platform/CSP of OSCE. In 2018/19 she started the project Women Vote Peace, focussing on the centenary of women's voting rights, bridging past, present and future commitment for peace and justice.

Maria Helena Nyberg

Born in Finland, she has been involved in multicultural and political issues since the beginning of her career as a certified translator and conference interpreter based in Switzerland. In 1980, her volunteer work started with the Anti-Apartheid Movement Switzerland; her commitment as long-time executive director and current editor-in-chief of the publications of the human rights organisation INCOMINDIOS brought her into contact with indigenous peoples around the world. At the UN, she advocates for conflict resolution and peace building, focusing on resource extraction and women's rights. In 1984, she was part of re-establishing the Swiss section of WILPF. She works for disarmament and a shift from military spending to civilian needs and co-organised the WomenVotePeace event in Zurich in 2019.

Giovanna Pagani

Has a long record in peace education, intercultural knowledge and gender equality. She lived for many years in Costa Rica and collaborated with universities and peace activists in Latin America with a focus on indigenous people, women and children. In 1989, has re-founded the Italian section of

WILPF and is honorary president. She has published several books and is active in anti-nuclear and disarmament movement, and on climat issues linked to peace.

Virginie Poyetton

Has a diploma in development studies from the graduate Institute, Geneva, Switzerland, Empirical Study in Media in development cooperation , Montevideo (Uruguay), Diploma in journalism, Centre de formation romand des journalistes, Lausanne (Switzerland, MA in information and communication from the Université Jean Moulin, Lyon, (France) and a thesis: Media and communication, Montréal (Canada). She has worked as a project manager and adviser in gender studies, Conflict Transformation and Human Rights and as a journaliste. Actually she works as Program Officer for gender and peace policy, for Christlicher Friedensdienst (cfd) in Switzerland.

Annemarie Sancar,

PhD, Social Anthropologist, feminist expert in topics at the interface of migration, development cooperation and peace policy, political activist in green and peace movements, experienced from 10 years in Swiss Development Cooperation, 3 years for swisspeace monitoring UNSCR 1325, 8 years as an elected member of municipality council in Bern, member of WIDE Women in Development Switzerland, of WILPF Switzerland and of the Working Group Gender Justice of Swiss Green Party.

Nina Sankari

Polish social activist, translator, journalist. She combines feminism, rationalism, humanism and atheism in her fight for freedom, equality, democracy and human emancipation. Nina Sankari publishes in Poland and abroad, ex. in Racjonalista.pl, Feminoteka, Fakty i Mity, La Raison, Egalité, 50/50, Regards de femmes, ResPublica, Charlie Hebdo. She is co-founder and editor of the "Atheist Review", the quarterly of the Kazimierz Łyszczynski Foudation of which she is vice-president. Selected by "Gazeta Wyborcza" as one of 50 courageous women 2018 who change the world for better. London Secular Conference Award Winner 2018 for women's rights and secularism. She is project partner in "Women vote Peace"

Gulnara Shahinian

Born in Yerevan, Armenia; studied English and Russian, gender and cultural studies at the European University in Budapest, Cambridge / USA, St. Petersburg/Russia, Yerevan and Stanford / USA and acquired further academic qualifications in conflict resolution, human rights and criminal law. She has worked on the Global Initiative Against Organized Crime, the UN Trust Fund on Slavery, as a Counselor of the Council of Europe and the International Labor Organization / ILO on trafficking in human beings, modern forms of slavery and forced labor. She has trained, published and participated as a key note speaker in international conferences. In 1996 she founded Democracy Today Armenia as a NGO focusing on peace building and conflict transformation, political engagement and elections.

Ingrid Sharp

is Professor of German Cultural and Gender History in the School of Languages, Cultures and Societies at the University of Leeds and is currently researching German opposition to the First World War. She has written several articles on the history of WILPF, including (2013) 'Feminist Peace Activism 1915 – 2010: Are We Nearly There Yet?' Peace and Change issue 2 volume 38, 155-180. Her co-edited volume with Matthew Stibbe Women Activists between War and Peace. Europe 1918-1923 was published by Bloomsbury in 2017.

Valentina Uspenskaya

is Associate Professor of Political Science at Tver' State University and Head of the Gender Studies and Women's History Centre, which she founded in 1999. Her research and teaching interests include feminism and politics of gender equality, women and politics in Russia, women's political thought, women's peace movement, civil society, comparative world politics, political anthropology. In 1996, she was a co-director of the First All-Russian Summer School in Women's and Gender Studies. In 2000-2002, she was a member of the Steering Committee of the Net of East-West Women (NEWW). She is an author of several international articles and co-editor of "Women and Transformation in Russia" (2013). In Russia, Uspenskaya has published extensively on women's/feminist history, women's political thought, gender equality policies, and particularly on Alexandra Kollontai's contribution into women's emancipation theory.

Sławomira Walczewska

PhD, feminist activist and philosopher. In 1999, Walczewska published Ladies, Knights and Feminists: Feminist Discourse in Poland, the book, who connected the current Polish feminists with their feminist grandmamas from the 19th century. In 1991 she co-founded the eFKa- Women's Foundation She edited the feminist magazine "Pełnym Głosem" (In Full Voice, 1993-1997) and was member of the editorial board of "Zadra" (1999 – 2018). In 2008 she was awarded by the Foundation Aufmüpfige Frauen von Dortmund. She lives in Krakow, Poland. She is project partner in "Women vote Peace" and organiser of historical-biographical Workshops „Jump over the Wall".

Perhaps,

we will see each other again

in 100 years,

to celebrate

peace